Jonathan Edwards

Jonathan Edwards
Art and the Sense of the Heart

TERRENCE ERDT

University of Massachusetts Press   Amherst

LC 80–5380
ISBN 0–87023–304–1
Printed in the United States of America
Library of Congress Cataloging in Publication Data
appear on the last printed page of this book.

A version of chapter one appeared in *Early Amer-
ican Literature* (Volume 13, 1978). Excerpts from
Number 251 of the "Miscellanies" of Jonathan
Edwards in the Beinecke Rare Book and Manu-
script Library are published by permission of the
Yale University Library.

To "LL" Willson

*The scholar loses no hour
which the man lives. . . .
What is lost in seemliness
is gained in strength.*

Ralph Waldo Emerson
The American Scholar

Contents

Preface

Jonathan Edwards has long been accorded a place in the front rank of colonial American writers; his aesthetics are now recognized as the primary characteristic of his theology; and his writings are judged worthy of extended literary analysis.[1] Oddly perhaps, no attempt has been made to discover if in his aesthetics Edwards attributes a particular significance to art. The discussion to follow contends that art as an instance of what he termed secondary beauty can perform a vital religious function by enabling the saint to conceive, and subsequently receive or revive, the particular emotional sensation that constitutes the religious experience—which Edwards referred to as the *sense of the heart*. My purpose in what is to follow is not to survey and to analyze Edwards' writings as works of art but to probe his aesthetic theory in order to discern the import he assigns to art.

A word about methodology is in order since it may seem to some readers slightly unorthodox. No one point of view—be it intellectual historical, literary, philosophical, or theological—assays adequately the ingredients of Edwards' system. He defended a Calvinist heritage that rapidly was losing primacy in his own country and had been long beset by sophisticated assailants abroad; he admired the new learning, and he was a man of letters. Not surprisingly, no one approach to his writings measures all their dimensions. While my orientation remains broadly literary in its objectives, necessarily I have had to borrow tools from several disciplines. The forays into intellectual history and Calvinist theology are intended to establish the foundation necessary for determining the implication of his aesthetics, not to serve as ends in themselves. I underscore my purpose and point of view, for Edwards enjoys the attention—as does Puritan studies in general—of intellectual historians, church historians, theologians, and students of sociology, philosophy, and even psychology; naturally each tends to guard the domain zealously as the prerogative of his or her discipline and to consider various questions as answerable only within its framework.[2] Although undoubtedly not entirely successful I have tried to avoid the liberty taken in some commentaries on Edwards, that offer an extended paraphrase, rather than a true exposition, and retain his own vocabulary even when it is most in need of explication. To establish a theological context for understanding the *sense of the heart,* a concept central to Edwards, I turn to the oft-slighted Calvin, who frequently is made to appear an ogre that delighted in terrifying our naive ancestors with grisly tableaux of hell-fire and endless torment. Not only is he misrepresented but ambiguously translated, such that the evolution of his *sensus suavitatis* has not been perceived. *Sense of the heart* is generally regarded as a memento of Edwards' reading of Locke, when in fact its origins trace back to the *Institutes.* Edwards reshaped the old conception, central to the doctrines of regeneration and assurance, into the cornerstone of his aesthetics.

Puritan writings, particularly journals and diaries, disclose a preoccupation with the question of what constitutes understanding of spiritual matters, of what distinguishes *speculative* from *heart* knowledge. The Calvinist wanted to record his epiphanies—the moments when he actually perceived the meaning of the Gospel message necessary for salvation. Thomas Shepard, for instance, never seemed to tire of repeating in his journal what the reader familiar with Puritan theology must regard as commonplace: "I saw . . . that Christ and myself were quite contrary. (1) As all my evil was in myself, so all my good was in Christ as sufficient. (2) As all my evil came from myself, so all my good from Christ as efficient. (3) As I spoiled and defaced all Christ's work, so Christ restored, repaired, and built it up." Behind Shepard's statement lies the assumption that two levels of understanding exist, one natural and the other supernatural. The first is based upon reason, the second upon the response of a regenerate will. When grace changes the "inclination," or capacity, of his will, Shepard can then respond: "And this did make Christ sweet unto me when I thus looked upon him, being thus come, and began to work some confidence in me of grace. Only I saw it was mercy only which moved him to succor."[3] Once his heart has been transformed, he can *see* mercy, feel in his heart the quality of mercy. Puritanism possessed an established lexicon to designate the epistemology, or psychology, of regeneration; such terms as *inclination, bias, experimental knowledge, sweetness,* and *heart* were the inheritance of Edwards. Shifting the emphasis of the new psychology from the understanding to the will, and further analyzing and broadening its category of ideas of reflection, he scrutinized regeneration with a thoroughness not possible to the Puritan commentators of the previous century. The substance of his explanation adhered to the Calvinist position, with a quite distinct and significant modification: the reaction of the sanctified heart, the feeling of sweetness, Edwards claimed to be essentially an aesthetic response, a reaction to, or perception of, spiritual beauty. A unique sense of beauty stands, he saw, as the sign of divinity, and offers assurance of one's election.

As did Calvin and many of the Puritan writers, Edwards found that the experience of the sense of sweetness is fleeting; its coming and going, the high and low points of religious experience, cannot be controlled or predicted. His reading of Locke, his knowledge of the new psychology led him to conclude that, needing something tangible to conceive of spirit, the mind may substitute images derived from its ideas of nature, from the fantasies of the imagination, or from works of art. The feeling of beauty evoked by such images can surrogate the sense of the heart, and thereby allow for a natural conception of divine beauty, or recall the sensation of spiritual beauty once it has faded.

Until the completion of the definitive Yale edition of Edwards' works, a variety of editions and reprints must be consulted. I have used the Yale editions where possible, otherwise have relied in the main upon the Williams and Parsons edition.

Several years ago, in a series of seminars at Santa Barbara, Lawrence Willson made so real and personally meaningful the subject of Puritanism in American cultural history, raised such intriguing questions, offering more challenges than answers, that, captivated, I've spent the last eight years happily absorbed in a labor that previously I would have thought dreadful. Many of the themes pursued in the following pages have evolved from my perception of his insights. To Everett Emerson particularly I am indebted also, for his enthusiasm and encouragement, practical advice, and for his ever generous sharing of his erudition in Puritan studies and American literature. One of the pleasures of the present undertaking has been the discovery of such kindness as his. I would also like to extend my appreciation to: Thomas A. Schafer, for generously making available his transcription of Edwards' "Miscellanies"; John E. Smith, who took time from his busy schedule to chat at length about the progress of the Yale edition of Edwards; Karl Keller, who provided a valuable critical reading of the manuscript; and Norman Fiering, who read an early version of the manuscript and, in long correspondence, argued vigorously the point of view of the intellectual historian—his own work on Edwards, it is to be hoped, soon will be forthcoming. Several librarians have made my task easier: particularly Carol Gibbens at the University of California, Santa Barbara, Library; Marjorie G. Wynne, Research Librarian, Yale University Library; Doris Smedes of the Huntington Library; Polly Pierce, Stockbridge Massachusetts Public Library; and the staff of the Berkeley Doe Library. I wish to thank Yale University Library for permission to quote from the unpublished "Miscellanies" held by the Beinecke Rare Book and Manuscript Library.

Several friends deserve acknowledgement for their encouragement and for the patience and endurance they displayed listening to me think aloud about a largely unfamiliar subject: Gillian Jennifer Wilson, Mashey Maurice Bernstein, Alan W. Howell, Peter H. Griffin, Torborg Lundell, Daryl Landon, Van Tibbels, and Alice O'Reilly.

Terrence Erdt
Berkeley, 1980

Jonathan Edwards

Chapter 1
The Calvinist Psychology
of the Heart

Scholars have often noted the central importance to Jonathan Edwards' thought of the *sense of the heart,* the special knowledge of spiritual matters possessed by the saint. Harold Simonson characterizes the *sense* as summarizing Edwards' whole system of thought;[1] and John E. Smith proposes that "no idea in all of Edwards' works is more original and no doctrine was more far reaching in its influence upon the course of Puritan piety."[2] Discussion of the term focuses generally upon its illustrating several of Edwards' debts: to the Cambridge Platonists, particularly John Smith and the theory of *spiritual sensation;*[3] to Francis Hutcheson and his treatise on the *moral sense;*[4] and finally to John Locke and the sensationalist psychology.[5] The last topic occasions perhaps the most extensive discussion, and the contention that the *sense* refers primarily to Locke's account of the origin of simple ideas has wide acceptance, in large measure because of Perry Miller's life of Edwards' mind.[6]

Miller took pains to convince his readers that Edwards' thought could best be defined as "Puritanism recast in the idiom of empirical psychology" (p. 62). Edwards, accordingly, spoke in the terminology of traditional Calvinism but meant something quite different —the empiricism of Newton and Locke. His writings were thus cryptic, and the key to their understanding, Miller argued, is to read them with the *Essay* in mind. Grace, for instance, as an historical concept received little elucidation in Miller's account; he was interested mainly in establishing that Edwards had translated the doctrine into the language of Locke. It was "a new simple idea"; any significance in its similarity to the traditional Calvinist doctrine paled before Edwards' striving to "emancipate Protestantism from the windingsheet of the Middle Ages (p. 256). The *sense of the heart* was above all else, Miller pronounced, "a perception, a form of apprehension derived exactly as Locke said mankind gets all simple ideas, out of sensory experience" (p. 139). By not discussing the *sense of the heart* apart from the new psychology, Miller gave the impression that the term derived solely from Edwards' reading of Locke and that it constituted an essentially new explanation of spiritual knowledge.

Conrad Cherry protested Miller's encouragement of an appreciation for Edwards "at points other than where traditional Calvinist tenets receive extensive treatment," maintaining instead that Edwards reclaimed a view of faith more central to early Calvinism than to Newtonian science.[7] Locke's theory that the mind was a simple entity possessing the powers of intellection and volition explained, as the old faculty psychology could not, how it was that the act of faith was, as indeed Calvinism had taught, a response of the whole man. In Cherry's view the *sense* is, however, a Lockean "simple idea," an elemental sensation consisting of "the harmonious interpenetration of the cognitive and volitional powers of the human agent" (p. 18). Locke's psychology, and in particular the theory of the *sense*, enabled Edwards in other words, to avoid the trap which had ensnared the early Puritan theologians, namely that of emphasizing alternately the intellect and then the will, in what supposedly was a single, unified experience (p. 13).

Recently William J. Scheick has remarked, quite correctly, that such expressions as *the sense of the heart* and the *sensible* effects of grace are not unique to Edwards; they, the term *inward sweetness,* and the image of honey, by which the latter is often represented, appear frequently in early Puritan writings, so that "the presence of these expressions in Edwards' work, consequently, cannot be readily attributed, as Perry Miller suggests, to Locke's influence."[8]

Sense as a designation for faith and knowledge of the heart enjoyed notable currency among seventeenth-century Puritans.[9] The term was central to what perhaps appropriately could be labeled a Calvinist psychology of the heart, that was available to Edwards, informing his view of regeneration as an aesthetic experience. To perceive the foundation of Edwards' theory in sixteenth- and seventeenth-century commentary on the saint's saving knowledge, two assumptions or conclusions first formulated by Miller and shared by many subsequent students of Edwards must be questioned. The first supposes an ineradicable rationalism within Puritanism because the only formal psychology available to represent regeneration was the scholastic faculty psychology. There supposedly was war between rationalism and piety:

> When he [Edwards] contended with Chauncy, he was fighting not only the rationalism of the Enlightenment, but the rationalism grafted onto the Aristotelian and Thomistic strain which had been transplanted to New England in the form of the first settlers' technologia. Calvin himself was the source of the difficulty: though he warned Protestantism against linking theology to psychological theories ... he riveted Calvinism to the medieval doctrine of the faculties. . . . There is no better epitome of the scholastic position than Calvin's: the office of the will is "to choose and follow what the understanding shall have pronounced to be good, to abhor and avoid what it shall have condemned."[10]

According to scholastic psychology, the will must blindly follow the last dictate of the understanding and therefore the Puritan had no choice, claimed Miller, but to make regeneration take place in the understanding, "because in all human conduct an understanding of some sort must precede any act of will, and thus grace itself must act upon the understanding. . . ." Grace was therefore, in Miller's view, an elevation of reason.[11]

Yet in the *Institutes of the Christian Religion,* and in many of the later Puritan documents, there is evidence that faculty psychology did not necessarily have such a rigid and destructive hold upon piety. The concept of the heart, which the Puritan took largely from his Bible, for him the divinely inspired source of information about spiritual matters, permitted impunity from the horns of the dilemma Miller saw threatening, namely the heresies of Pelagianism or Arminianism: either the will followed regenerate reason automatically, so that religion was an affair of the intellect, or it could choose to neglect the determinations of enlightened reason.[12] The concept of the heart influenced the writings of even the most rationalistic of Puritans. John Preston, for instance, who seems to have favored a theology laced with an uncommon emphasis upon reason, underscored the importance of a regenerate heart if reasoned discourse were to have effect:

A man may be able to shew an object, and to bring it to light: but what if the eye be amisse, the man is not able to see and to discerne for all that: If a mans eye be blind, if there be any weft in it, he is not able to remove it: So a man may propound arguments, but to make the heart capable of those arguments, he may propound reasons and perswasions, but to make the heart apprehensive of them, it is above the power of the Creature.[13]

It was commonplace in Puritan tracts to distinguish the conduct of the saint from that of the classical Greek paragon of virtue, who lived according to reason, by insisting that the saint's heart was different; although in each case the will followed the last dictate of the understanding, the saint's action resulted from a different inclination. This was the important point. The rankest hypocrite might somehow manage a change in conduct, though it were unlikely, but only God could alter the disposition of the heart. There could be virtue only if the individual's motivation, or inclination, were righteous.

Edwards' theory of the sense of the heart relied upon the traditional teaching on the heart and its function in *saving knowledge*. The sense of the heart for Edwards was not an idea and an emotional response joined, as has been assumed.[14] Instead he held that an emotion, such as that experienced in reaction to spiritual matters, could function virtually as an apprehension. The same peculiarity of the will's functioning in a manner that from the perspective of faculty psychology would be attributed to the understanding, characterized Calvin's and many Puritans' expositions of the psychology of faith. The divines assembled at Westminster (1643–47) prefaced their confession of faith by commending "not a brain-knowledge, a mere speculation; this may be in the worst of men, nay, in the worst of creatures, the devils themselves, and that in such an eminency, as the best of saints cannot attain to in this life of imperfection; but an inward, a savoury, an heart knowledge, such as was in that martyr, who, though she could not dispute for Christ, could die for him. This is that spiritual sense and feeling of divine truths the Apostle speaks of, Heb.v.14, *Having your senses exercised,* &c."[15]

I

The concept of the heart remains a mystery to students of Puritanism, although instances of its use and evidence of its importance abound. John Winthrop accounted for the migration to the New World with: "When God intendes a man to a worke he setts a Byas on his heart so as tho' he be tumbled this way and that yet his Bias still drawes him to that side, and there he restes at last."[16] Thomas Hooker wrote that "a broken and humble heart, either lies right, or will come right, it will come to that bent of the Rule that is revealed."[17] In terms of the heart Thomas Shepard explained the sequence of events leading to his conversion; hearing John Preston preach, "the Lord so bored my ears as that I understood what he spake and the secrets of my soul were laid upon before me—the hypocrisy of all my good things I thought I had in me—as if one had told him of all that ever I did, of all the turnings and deceits of my heart, insomuch as that I thought he was the most searching preacher in the world. And I began to love him much and to bless God I did see my frame and my hypocrisy and self and secret sins, although I found a hard heart and could not be affected with them."[18]

The meaning of the heart for Calvinists derived from Biblical usage, by which it designates, nebulously, "the inner essence of the whole man, the battleground of God and the devil.[19] Calvinists often let the term stand in its Biblical obscurity, but the awesome subject of regeneration sometimes necessitated that they pinpoint a particular significance. They tried to find an equivalent in faculty psychology and generally identified the heart with the will, the source of emotions, or *affections* as they were called—such feelings as love and hate. But to preserve the tenor of Biblical teaching, or at least their perception of it, they found it necessary to modify slightly the existing psychology. The heart, or will, by nature is disposed, or inclined, or (as in the examples from Winthrop and Hooker) bent or biased. Edward Taylor summed up the point in a meditation:

> I fain would praise thee, Lord, but when I would,
>   I finde my Sin my Praise dispraises bring.
> I fain would lift my hands up as I should,
>   But when I do, I finde them fould by Sin.
> I strive to heave my heart to thee, but finde
> When striving, in my heart an heartless minde.

Oh! that my Love, and mine Affections rich
    Did spend themselves on thee and thou hadst them.
I strive to have thy Glory on them pitch
    And fetch thee them. Hence Solomon thy jem,
And glorious Type thy Sparkling Beams out flings
But in the same my Love but little springs.[20]

Such attention to the will's inherent proclivity, over which neither sinner nor saint had control, as a matter of emphasis was foreign to scholastic psychology. The sinner could desperately want to love God, but the inclination of his heart would not permit him to unless it were transformed through grace. Doctrinally the disposition of the heart was immensely significant to Calvinism, for it represented the moral cast of the mind, the essential motivation of the individual spiritually considered. Damnation or salvation hung upon the direction of the will. In discussion of freedom of the will, inclination was, from Calvin's point of view, the deciding factor. Man sins necessarily because of the will's inherent disposition, but sins voluntarily all the same; the will freely wills what it wills—the theme Edwards developed in his great *Enquiry.* The bias of the will results in man's love of self, which is pride.

The Puritan rehearsed over and over the doctrine of the heart's inclination. Anxiously he tried to discover the *frame* of his mind. In despair he found that his motivations were despicably selfish and that he was powerless to change them, that only a divine influence could direct his true feelings to God. Thomas Shepard recorded in his diary on October 7, 1643:

> On Sabbath morning I saw more of my own heart, viz., that God's rules did not only lead me but my own ends in attendance upon them. And hence I saw I was not led by the Spirit, for I was unwilling to submit to a rule by casting away my profit or honor, etc. But I came to Christ to act me and not only to show me his will but to incline my heart to it and to give me power to do it, to live in me blessedly and comfortable.[21]

Anticipating Edwards, William Fenner in his *A Treatise of the Affections* explained that "you must have this same new heart, otherwise ye cannot set your affections on God. For there is a heart that will set its affections on God, and there is a heart that will not."[22]

In the *Institutes* Calvin found that the psychology of the Schoolmen did not explain altogether satisfactorily the change in inclination that occurs in regeneration. Though annoyed by the subtleties with which the philosophers made divisions and subdivisions in classifying the powers of the soul, he declared that for the purposes of piety it was best to hold that *soul* designates the understanding and the will—or understanding and heart (he used heart and will for the most part interchangeably). "Not to entangle ourselves in useless questions," he granted "that the understanding is, as it were, the leader and governor of the soul; and that the will is always mindful of the bidding of the understanding, and in its own desires awaits the judgment of the understanding."[23]

Nevertheless Calvin was aware of the danger of rationalism lurking in the unqualified acceptance of faculty psychology. He noted that the Socratic and scholastic philosophers in subordinating the will to the understanding "always imagine reason in man as that faculty whereby he may govern himself aright" (I.xv.6–7). Yet (contrary perhaps to popular belief) he did not go to the other extreme and deny the potency of reason; he did not teach that the Fall had resulted in a drastic and debilitating change in the faculty of the understanding *per se*. The power of reason indeed was diminished, he held, but was nevertheless intact, as could be seen in the formidable accomplishments of the world's great jurists, orators, and scientists.[24] Reason was one of man's "natural" gifts and as such it remained, unlike the "supernatural" gifts, after the Fall.

When Calvin charged that the powers of understanding and judgment were "plunged into deep darkness," he did not mean there was an inability to reason correctly.

> When we so condemn human understanding for its perpetual blindness as to leave it no perception of any object whatever, we not only go against God's Word, but also run counter to the experience of common sense. For we see implanted in human nature some sort of desire to search out the truth to which man would not at all aspire if he had not already savoured it. Human understanding then possesses some power of perception, since it is by nature captivated by love of truth. The lack of this endowment in brute animals proves their nature gross and irrational. Yet this longing for truth, such as it is, languishes before it enters upon its race because it soon falls into vanity [*vanitatem*, pride].
> (II.ii.12)

Only in contemplating spiritual matters did the intellect perform feebly. Because of the change in the inclination of the will as a consequence of the Fall, there was love only of self—vanity; and without the love of God the love of truth comes to naught in trying to understand the world of the spirit. Thus spiritual matters do not really interest the unregenerate mind, not enough for it to pursue and confront them, and since it does not experience them it can only possess an abstract, or speculative knowledge.

Man's blindness to the realm of spirit owes not simply to aberrations in judgment resulting from his sensuality. The Fall corrupted the whole of man's soul but mainly the heart or will. "It is pointless and foolish," Calvin emphasized, "to restrict the corruption that arises thence [from the Fall] only to what are called the impulses of the senses; or to call it the 'kindling wood' that attracts, arouses, and drags into sin only that part which they term 'sensuality' " (II.i.9). The fundamental corruption of human nature, he repeated several times in the *Institutes,* citing a plenitude of Scriptural passages, lies in the heart's being given over to pride. Loss of the right inclination of will causes in turn the depravity or dullness of the intellect.

Faith Calvin defined as a knowledge beyond that of the understanding and a certitude beyond what reason can provide. It was a knowledge free of rationalism.

> Such, then, is a conviction that requires no reasons; such, a knowledge with which the best reason agrees—in which the mind reposes more securely and constantly then in any reasons; such, finally, a feeling that can be born only of heavenly revelation [*talis denique sensus, qui nisi ex coelesti revelatione nasci nequeat*]. I speak of nothing other than what each believer experiences within himself—though my words fall beneath a just explanation of the matter. . . . Let us, then, know that the only true faith is that which the Spirit of God seals in our hearts. (I.vii.5)

Faculty psychology to an important extent proved wanting in explaining faith, for it confined knowledge to the understanding and the process of arriving at knowledge to the operation of reason. But Paul had written: "For with the heart man believeth unto righteousness, and with the mouth man confesseth to salvation."[25] Accordingly Calvin, perhaps influenced by Augustine,[26] spoke of the *sense of divinity;* Benjamin Warfield explains: "such a sense discovers divinity only where divinity is and only by a perception of it"; with "the newly implanted spiritual sense the saint could discern the stamp of divinity upon Scripture."[27]

Perhaps of more importance to later Calvinist teaching on faith is not Calvin's metaphor of a special sense organ but his repeated mention of a unique emotional feeling, or sense, as the essence of faith. He refers to the seal of the Spirit as an interior feeling: *sed interioris affectus sciamus esse testimonia* (III.xii.7), and in his commentary on Paul's letter to the Romans he speaks of *ex communi piorum omnium sensum,* a feeling or perception common to all the pious.[28] Generally in the *Institutes* Calvin uses the Latin *sensus* to signify the unique feeling constituting faith. Unfortunately *sensus* has several possible meanings in English and has consequently been rendered with latitude: so much so that the continuity of the term in the *Institutes* is lost sight of and its use among Puritan writers unperceived. In the third book of the *Institutes,* to take one example, Calvin writes that God touches the sinner with a *sensus* of his goodness so that he will despair of his own works and depend upon God's mercy. Then comes: *Hic est fidei sensus, per quem peccator in possessionem venit suae salutis. . . .* (This is the sense of faith, through which the sinner comes into possession of his salvation).[29] The four principal English translations of the *Institutes* respectively render *sensus* here as *feeling, sentiment, experience,* and *meaning* (in his own French translation Calvin wrote *le sentiment*).[30] The sense, or feeling, distinguished, Calvin declared, real faith from that expounded by the Schoolmen. The Scholastics insisted that the authenticity of Scripture rested upon rational proof, but this was no more than an assent of "cold reason." Faith contained a persuasion that was more vital to the recipient than whatever reason could muster. Early in the *Institutes* Calvin outlined his position on the testimony of the Spirit, distinguishing it from an illumination of reason.

> Since for unbelieving men religion seems to stand by opinion alone, they, in order not to believe anything foolishly or lightly, both wish and demand rational proof that Moses and the prophets spoke divinely. But I reply: the testimony of the Spirit is more excellent than all reason. For as God alone is a fit witness of himself in his Word, so also the Word will not find acceptance in men's hearts before it is sealed by the inward testimony of the Spirit. The same Spirit, therefore, who has spoken through the mouths of the prophets must penetrate into our hearts to persuade us that they faithfully proclaimed what had been divinely commanded. (I.vii.4)

For the saint faith proved to have a momentous personal relevance in a way no mere abstraction ever could. Calvinists for generations rehearsed the same steps, the preparation, for salvation. The attempt to live up to the moral code of the Commandments so far surpassed the natural ability of the saint that he became convinced of the impossibility of his effecting his own salvation. In desperation therefore he turned to the Scriptures. Then the fear of damnation and the humiliation of knowing his spiritual helplessness brought him to appreciate the promises of salvation offered by the Word. With damnation for eternity in the balance the promises were awesomely significant.

> . . . Since our hearts cannot, in God's mercy, either seize upon life ardently enough or accept it with the gratefulness we owe, unless our minds are first struck and overwhelmed by fear of God's wrath and by dread of eternal death, we are taught by Scripture to perceive that apart from Christ, God is, so to speak, hostile to us, and his hand is armed for our destruction; to embrace his benevolence and father love in Christ alone. (II.xvi.2)

The saint possessed a special power of perception. In those areas of Scripture that present promises of salvation the saint perceived that "the undoubted power of his [God's] divine majesty lives and breathes there" (I.vii.5). On the other hand, to the unregenerate, as Paul wrote (I Cor. 2:14), the things of the Spirit were foolishness. Unless the Holy Spirit instilled the special *sensus*, the Biblical promises held little meaning and were accorded relative indifference. "Indeed, the Word of God is like the sun, shining upon all those to whom it is proclaimed, but with no effect among the blind. Now, all of us are blind by nature in this respect. Accordingly, it cannot penetrate into our minds unless the Spirit, as the inner teacher, through his illumination makes entry for it" (III.ii.34).

The sense given to the saint provided actual experience of the spiritual nature of what otherwise was known only intellectually. The saint acquired an *experimental* knowledge, for he *tasted* (the standard term among Puritans, and with Edwards) a divine quality: "And man's understanding, thus beamed by the light of the Holy Spirit, then at last truly begins to taste [*gustare incipit*] those things which belong to the Kingdom of God, having formerly been quite foolish and dull in tasting them" (III.ii.34).

What did Calvin mean in saying that the saint actually experienced or tasted something of divinity, and what indeed was perceived? These are difficult questions; yet we are hard put to make sense of much of Calvinist and Puritan discourse without answers to them, for we are dealing, as in the case of the heart, with basic terms.

Calvin's explanation that the sense of the heart is the particular feeling with which the saint reacts to the message of salvation was not a pietistic vagary. He precisely labeled the feeling *suavitas,* sweetness, which Edwards, and many Puritans before him, incorporated into a lexicon to describe the religious experience. The saint, knowing well that he deserves damnation and that morally he is incapable of fulfilling the laws of God, feels a unique sweetness, or delight, in hearing the promise Christ offered. "But there is a far different feeling of full assurance that in the Scriptures is always attributed to faith. It is this which puts beyond doubt God's goodness clearly manifested for us. But that cannot happen without our truly feeling its sweetness [*suavitatem*] and experiencing it in ourselves" (III.ii.15). The grace of the Holy Spirit enables the saint in the throes of humiliation and fear to perceive a tremendous power reflected or visible in the Word. The perception is the taste of a divine quality, "the sure experience of godliness," a "practical knowledge [*practica notitia*] . . . doubtless more certain and firmer than any idle speculation" (I.xiii.13–14). The power the saint tastes is of God's mercy towards him. Calvin maintained that the attributes of God known through Scripture when grace is present are those "by which he is shown to us not as he is in himself, but as he is toward us" (I.x.2). The attributes were vivid experience to the saint of God's goodness and mercy, and they were known by means of the feeling in his heart.

For the feeling of *suavitas* the saint feels in hearing the promise of salvation is the sign God cares for him, has chosen him for salvation. The feeling itself is the saint's firsthand knowledge of God's mercy. And thus it is, to answer our question, that the perception or taste is his own emotional reaction of gratitude. It is the response after the Holy Spirit changes the heart's inclination. Then the heart has the capacity to respond to spiritual matters. The feeling is an inward revelation. Its presence indicates God's mercy, and experiencing it constitutes unique knowledge of God's mercy and of one's own election. But because of its basis in inward feeling, it is knowledge known *experimentally,* through individual experience. Thus the difference between the philosophers' speculative knowledge of God's mercy and that known experientially by the saint is the "earnest feeling of grace [*serio . . . gratiae sensu*] which [Paul] commends, because they do not at all taste God's special care, by which alone his fatherly favor is known" (*qui a specialem Dei curam, ex qua demum cognoscitur paternus eius favor, minime gustant,* I.xvi.1).

According to Calvin, the God who exhibits a fatherly favor is, in a manner of speaking, one of two gods the saint comes to know. At first the saint perceives through Scripture only the God hostile to fallen man, his enemy because of unrighteousness, the God of vengeance. Once enabled to have the sense of the heart, however, the saint sees the God of mercy, who "is moved by pure and freely given love of us to receive us into grace," who by Christ's expiation wipes away man's evil (II.xvi.1–3). This God Calvin refers to as a kindly father, and it is he whom man discovers in the feeling of *suavitas*. Faith rests in the discovery, then, of God's mercy, the discovery of Christ, the comprehensible image of the loving father, the accommodation to the measure of finite minds (II.vi.4).

The sense of *suavitas* is essential to faith in Calvin's scheme. It signals the presence of the divine quality of mercy embodied in Christ; it is the experience or contact with "the true image of his [God the Father's] benefits." It is the response to the "splendor of Christ" (*fulgor Christi,* III.ii.1). Once the saint through the power of the Holy Spirit tastes the splendor, or excellency, of God's mercy, love is aroused in him.

> But how can the mind be aroused to taste the divine goodness without at the same time being wholly kindled to love God in return? For truly, that abundant sweetness [*suavitatis affluentia*] which God has stored up for those who fear him cannot be known without at the same time powerfully moving us. And once anyone has been moved by it, it utterly ravishes him and draws him to itself. Therefore, it is no wonder if a perverse and wicked heart never experiences that emotion [*affectus*] by which, borne up to heaven itself, we are admitted to the most hidden treasures of God and to the most hallowed precincts of his kingdom, which should not be defiled by the entrance of an impure heart. (III.ii.41)

The love which the saint feels after experiencing *suavitas* Calvin sometimes called a *relish* or *keenness,* terms later popular among

Puritan writers. The regenerative change in the inclination of the heart effects "a new keenness [*aciem*], as it were, to contemplate the heavenly mysteries, whose splendor had previously blinded it" (III.ii.34).

Possession of the sense of the heart constitutes the assurance of election. It is an *exclusive testimony* enjoyed by the saint alone. The experience is so marked that there can be no doubt of one's salvation: the feeling of *suavitas* provides the mind with "a clear knowledge of the divine will toward itself."[31] So awesome is the feeling, the saint realizes it must be of divine origin. Knowing that the feeling signifies God's power, the saint trusts the Biblical promise that Christ will save him; the "feeling of full assurance . . . puts beyond doubt God's goodness" (III.ii.15). So it is that the promise of salvation penetrates the saint's heart.

The sense of *suavitas* is, however, elusive. The saint may one day experience the sense of the heart to the point of euphoria but the next day be again near despair in fear of damnation. Even the saint can question his election, Calvin conceded, but there is never a total disbelief. No certainty is free of all doubts and anxiety. There can be no perfect faith in this life, he opined, because of the division between flesh and spirit. A complex chain of factors in human psychology is the reason: "the godly heart feels in itself a division because it is partly imbued with sweetness from its recognition of the divine goodness, partly grieves in bitterness from an awareness of its calamity; partly rests upon the promise of the gospel, partly trembles at the evidence of its own iniquity" (III.ii.18). The important point, Calvin stressed, is that the feeling of assurance is never lost entirely; "the end of the conflict [between faith and doubt] is always this: that faith ultimately triumphs over those difficulties which besiege and seem to imperil it" (III.ii.18). The sense is fugitive but never more than temporarily lost. Its departures and recurrences train the saint to depend upon God rather than self: "the very sweetness and delightfulness of grace so fills a man who is cast down in himself with fear, and at the same time with admiration, that he depends upon God and humbly submits himself to his power" (III.ii.23).

The sense of the heart is a higher or, as it was often called, a *saving* knowledge; Calvin considered it to be a secret revelation made only to the saint.[32] From the point of view of faculty psychology it is somewhat absurd to say that a feeling constitutes a special knowledge, for knowledge belongs to the realm of the understanding, while emotions pertain to the will. The affections are involved in choice, not in apprehension. Yet the sense of *suavitas* for the saint is the means by which the mercy of God is known, as heat is known by the sense of touch. While sometimes the reprobate has a feeling similar to the saint's of the Gospel's power so that he stands convinced of his election, he lacks the supreme confidence and trust. Calvin more particularly defined the saint's heart knowledge when he distinguished it from the ordinary knowledge described in faculty psychology: "When we call faith 'knowledge' we do not mean comprehension of the sort that is commonly concerned with those things which fall under human sense perception. For faith is so far above sense that man's mind has to go beyond and rise above itself in order to attain it." The knowledge of faith distinctly differs from ordinary knowledge, he pointed out, because it includes certitude. "Even where the mind has attained, it does not comprehend what it feels. But while it is persuaded of what it does not grasp, by the very certainty of its persuasion it understands more than if it perceived anything human by its own capacity" (III.ii.14). The foundation for the complete certitude of faith lies in its experiential or experimental character. At times the saint directly perceives the object of his faith, which for him then ceases to be a remote abstraction. The feeling of *suavitas* presents a glimpse of the power of God's mercy. The reprobate might *know* God as merciful but the saint *feels* his mercy. Therefore faith is knowledge that consists in "assurance rather than in comprehension"; it requires "full and fixed certainty, such as men are wont to have from things experienced and proved." Many people are capable of an intellectual conviction that God is merciful:

> But there is a far different feeling of full assurance that in the Scriptures is always attributed to faith. It is this which puts beyond doubt God's goodness clearly manifested for us. But that cannot happen without our truly feeling its sweetness and experiencing it in ourselves [*Id autem fieri nequit, quin eius suavitatem vere sentiamus, et experiamur in nobis ipsis*]. (III.ii.15)

To know God's mercy there must be the capacity to respond with a certain emotion. The saint, because the inclination of his will is changed, feels *suavitas* in hearing the promises of salvation. He thereby acquires an experiential knowledge of the nature of God and of divine providence, about which the reprobate by comparison knows nothing.

Calvin seems hesitant over whether or not, in terms of faculty psychology, the illumination of the saint should be classified as belonging to the understanding or to the will. Occasionally he speaks of the illumination of the mind and at other times of the illumination of the heart.[33] The ambiguity may have resulted from the strangeness, from the point of view of scholastic psychology, of having an emotion constitute an apprehension. But Calvin went on to attribute to the understanding the act of tasting or experiencing the sense and then to emphasize that it was the heart or will in which confidence existed.

> But if it is true that the mind's real understanding is illumination by the Spirit of God, then in such confirmation of the heart his power is much more clearly manifested, to the extent that the heart's distrust is greater than the mind's blindness. It is harder for the heart to be furnished with assurance than for the mind to be endowed with thought. The Spirit accordingly serves as a seal, to seal up in our hearts those very promises the certainty of which it has previously impressed upon our minds. (III.ii.36)

Thus Calvin classified the apprehension of God's mercy, as known through the feeling of *suavitas,* with the understanding and the trust and assurance resulting from that feeling to the heart. The important point for the purpose of seeing the context for Edwards' version of the sense of the heart is that an emotion or affection is the source of spiritual knowledge, that the sense of the heart is virtually an apprehension. The sense was at best awkwardly represented through faculty psychology, yet it could be described according to the scholastic system without, contrary to Miller's theory, reduction to rationalism. A feeling in the heart or will becomes an idea in the understanding, to which in turn there is a reaction of the will in the form of love. The process Calvin depicted emphasized the will in order to preserve the Biblical concept of the heart as the basis for faith. Seventeenth-century Puritans very often reflected something of the same concern. And while it is beyond the scope of the present discussion to pursue thoroughly their interest in the sense of the heart, a few illustrations from their writings will serve to establish some of the main points of the tradition to which Jonathan Edwards was heir.

II

Several historians oppose Perry Miller's characterization that grace became reason elevated among the seventeenth-century Puritans and claim instead that there were actually two psychological positions contending in the accounts of regeneration.[34] The "intellectualist" stance held that the understanding presents to the will what is to be embraced or rejected, the will desiring as the understanding judges; accordingly, the will must follow the last dictate of the understanding. Because of error in the intellect, often caused by unruly passions or faulty reasoning, the will may choose the apparent rather than the real good. Milton summed up the intellectualist theory, which had been advanced by Aquinas and Bellarmine, with Michael's saying to Adam: "Reason in man obscured, or not obey'd, / Immediately inordinate desires / And upstart passions catch the Government / From Reason. . . ."[35] Because the will is determined by the last judgment of the practical intellect, human conduct, according to the intellectualist scheme, is largely a matter of the commands of reason.

In opposition stood the "voluntarist" position, not entirely contrary to scholasticism, which accorded the will the power of self-determination; in this scheme the will may reject the dictates of the understanding. At times, according to Norman Fiering, scholastic voluntarism combined with the Augustinian tradition, wherein the disposition or moral quality of the heart determines one's spiritual fate.[36] William Ames is often cited as an example of the Augustinian-voluntarist conception because of his making faith a matter of the will. In his famous *Marrow*, which was to become the standard textbook of theology at early Harvard and Yale, he wrote:

> Faith is the resting of the heart on God, the author of life and eternal salvation. . . . To believe signifies ordinarily an act of the understanding as it gives assent to evidence. But since as a consequence the will is wont to be moved and reach out to embrace the good thus proved, faith may rightly designate this act of the will as well. So it is to be understood in this book. . . . It is an act of choice, an act of the whole man—which is by no means a mere act of the intellect.[37]

Ames emphasized that the will is the primary object of grace and that the enlightenment of the mind alone is insufficient for regeneration. Surrendering oneself to Christ through faith, he declared, making a distinction Edwards later found useful, involves not so much an assent of the understanding as a consent of the will (1.iii.18).

Attention to the doctrine of the sense of the heart appears, as to be expected, more commonly among the voluntarists than the intellectualists. John Wollebius, whose *The Abridgement of Christian Divinity* in the 1670s replaced Ames' *Medulla* at Harvard, reiterated Calvin's description of the sign of the presence of divinity, the experience of the feeling of *suavitas:* "he knoweth more assuredly the Scriptures to be Gods Word, who hath tasted its sweetnesse, then he who gives credit to the Church witnessing this sweetnesse. . . ."[38] Wollebius also followed Calvin in regarding the taste as illumination of the mind; Ross, the translator of the *Abridgement,* uses the word *excellency,* the term Edwards adopted, to describe the quality perceived through redemption (p. 247). Many Puritans also stressed that through the sense of the heart the saint encounters that to which he assents intellectually; it supplies contact with a divine quality— the basis for the *intuitive* or *experimental* knowledge of spiritual matters. In *The Spiritual Taste Described,* Robert Dingley explained that:

> We taste God by faith, and particular applications of Christ unto the soule. For where there is tasting, there must be touching and applying the food. In other senses, as feeling, hearing, there must be a medium between the object and organ, not so in tasting. The thing tasted must be touched. Tis so here in this spiritual taste, there must be an application of Christ, and union with him by faith, and a grounded perswasion of his goodnesse to us, or wee can never taste him: To ponder Gods goodness in himselfe and to others is not all, but to bring it home and weigh his goodnesse to me, as, 1 Tim. 1.15. and Gal. 2.20. Oh tis this raises so sweet a relish in the heart. . . . Now faith applyes that goodnesse and sweetnesse that is in God, to a mans own soule in particular. . . . They know nothing yet as they ought to know, and, as the truth is in Jesus, till they have the Spirit, and by him have tasted how good the Lord is, till they have warm affections in heavenly things, and the bent and purpose of their hearts is to please God, and work by rule.[39]

Elaborating upon the standard distinction in Calvinism between speculative and saving knowledge, Richard Sibbes noted that "carnal man . . . though he have never so much knowledge . . . hath only notional knowledge, discoursive knowledge." The saint, he pointed out, has "a knowledge with a taste. . . . God gives the knowledge *per modum gustus*. When things are to us as in themselves, then things have a sweet relish. . . ." The saint perceives the God of mercy through the Word by his own response: "How do you know the word to be the word? It carrieth proof and evidence in itself. It is an evidence that the fire is hot to him that feeleth it, and that the sun shineth to him that looks on it; how much more doth the word. . . . I am sure I felt it, it warmed my heart, and converted me."[40] The feeling the Word effects in the saint differs from any other, numerous Puritan writers declared, so that one who has not experienced it has no clear idea of it. Typically the expositor of the uniqueness of the sense made an analogy to the taste of honey. Wollebius, for instance, affirmed that the saint recognizes God's word from its sweetness, just "as he who hath tasted honey himself, hath a more sure knowledge of its sweetnesse than he that believeth another speaking and witnessing of it."[41] Richard Baxter summarized much of the doctrine of the sense of the heart when he wrote:

> I do, therefore, neither despise evidence as unnecessary, nor trust to it alone as the sufficient total cause of my belief: for if God's grace do not open mine eyes, and come down in power upon my will, and insinuate into it a sweet acquaintance with the things unseen, and a taste of their goodness to delight my soul, no reasons will serve to stablish and comfort me, how undeniable soever.

> The way to have the firmest belief of the Christian faith is to draw near and taste, and try it, and lay bare the heart to receive the impression of it, and then, by the sense of its admirable effects, we shall know that which bare speculation could not discover. Though there must be a belief on other grounds first, so much as to let in the word into the soul, and to cause us to submit our hearts to its operations, yet it is this experience that must strengthen it, and confirm it. 'If any man do the will of Christ, he shall know that his doctrine is of God.' (John vii.17). The melody of music is better known by hearing it, than by reports of it; and the sweetness of meat is known better by tasting, than by hearsay; though upon report we may be drawn to taste and try. So is there a spiritual sense in us of the effects of the Gospel on our own hearts, which will cause men to love it, and hold it fast against the cavils of deceivers, or the temptations of the great deceiver.[42]

Though pointing emphatically to the affectional sense as the basis of faith, Baxter nevertheless illustrates the trend among seventeenth-century Calvinists of emphasizing the necessity of laying a ground-work of "rational apprehension" in order for it to occur. Calvin supposed a knowledge of the Scriptures as the *sine qua non* for the reception of the sense but continually underscored the simplicity of faith, its being fundamentally a matter of the Commandments and the promises of salvation. The Puritans, however, produced complex sums, compendiums, bodies, and abridgments of the principles of religion, organized dichotomously by the system of Ramus as an aid to memorization. Once the principles of religion were memorized, the saint was *prepared*, at least in part, to experience the sense of the heart.[43]

The sense was expected to be the sure sign of election, and it was spoken of so often in Puritan circles that those who had not experienced it were of course well aware of its existence and of the remarkable emotional response that marked its presence. Thomas Hooker warned that some who await the sense may expect too much because they "judge Christs presence by our one sense, and by some extraordinary sweetnesse that the soule imagins should be with him if Christ were there. This is the nature of every poore creature: he sets up a kind of imagination in his owne head, and thinkes if Christ were come once, there would be extraordinary sweetnesse and joy. Now setting up this imagination in his owne conceit, he will heare no other evidence if he cannot find this, and so mis-judgeth the presence of Christ."[44]

Hooker's admonition may be a sign of piety on the wane: the sense of the heart as Calvin presented it is an experience not to be matched, let alone surpassed; to suggest that the imagination could conceive of something that might overshadow the real sense of the heart possibly signals the death rattle of the pietistic verve that characterized preceding generations. While the transcendent character of the sense tends, by comparison with Calvin's representation, to be somewhat slighted as Puritan writers began to emphasize that one might *prepare* for regeneration, it should be noted that the feeling of *suavitas* continued to signify the presence of grace in the heart. They represented the elusiveness of the sense much as Calvin had, referring to the feeling as a brief *earnest*, or glimpse, of the experience to be enjoyed in heaven. The *Westminster Confession* spoke of "the inward evidence of those graces unto which these promises are made, the testimony of the Spirit of adoption witnessing with our spirits that we are the children of God, which Spirit is the earnest of our inheritance, whereby we are sealed to the day of redemption"(pp. 76–77).

My purpose in the preceding pages has been to point to what to some extent was part of a standard lexicon among Calvinists. It provided the foundation or starting point for certain oft-encountered conceptions in the writings of Jonathan Edwards, such as the sense of the heart, sweetness, and excellency. Historians sometimes have been impatient with Puritan piety and in exasperation over its seeming lack of intellectual sophistication have been prone to make Edwards, to say nothing of his forebears, hurriedly don the garb of the enlightenment. The consequence has been attributions to Locke which more rightly are due Augustine and Calvin. The assumption prevails in many studies of Edwards that the notion of the sense of the heart derives solely from Locke. Edwards' comparisons between the sense of the sweetness of divine things and the taste of honey are often taken as a sign of his dependence upon Locke, who used an occasional melliferous image. But as we have seen, the sense of the heart was fundamental in Calvinism; indeed it designated the religious experience itself. It was the state or frame of mind that constituted the saint's experience of grace, his exposure to and participation in spirit. Edwards, however, should not be thought of as being merely the passive recipient and uninspired perpetuator of the long established doctrine distinguishing speculative from saving knowledge, and it would be equally erroneous to regard his reading of Locke as unimportant to his conception of the sense of the heart. He viewed the mind and the influence of grace upon it in the light of the new psychology. Locke furnished him with new tools to probe the regenerate mind, and his psychological analysis resulted in significant departures from, or expansions of, traditional Calvinism. As the result of his sophistication in the new learning, he analyzed the gracious mind empirically and, having come to a more precise understanding of *suavitas* than had been possible in the days of faculty psychology, discovered new means to the reception of the sense of the heart, one of which was the feeling of beauty in response to a work of art.

Chapter 2
Edwards on the Sense
of the Heart

In its description of the mind, Locke's *Essay* fails in a significant respect, Jonathan Edwards decided, apparently not long after his first acquaintance with the work; it neglects to include as a vital element of psychology the heart. Possibly the full import of the omission did not occur to him in his first excited reading; initially he agreed that personal identity, the determination of the self as an independent entity, rests, as Locke declared, solely in thinking or consciousness, and he wrote in his notes:

> Well might Mr. Locke say that identity of person consisted in identity of consciousness, for he might have said that identity of spirit, too, consisted in the same consciousness. For a mind or spirit is nothing else but consciousness and what is included in it. The same consciousness is, to all intents and purposes, individually the very same spirit or substance as much as the same particle of matter can be the same with itself at different times.[1]

Later, however, he came to see the mistake. "Identity of person," he wrote in a subsequent entry, "is what seems never yet to have been explained." It is not, as Locke implied, merely having the same ideas from a past to a present moment and knowing by means of memory that they have been possessed previously. God could create two beings conscious of the same ideas, yet their minds would not be necessarily identical. They could "be in a very different state, one in a state of enjoyment and pleasure, and the other in a state of great suffering and torment."[2] Locke tended to ignore the will, the feelings, as he defined the term, of pleasure and pain experienced in reaction to one's ideas. He was oblivious to the cast of the mind, the heart, which determined what one could feel about something, whether it be natural or supernatural.

Nevertheless, Edwards viewed Locke's psychology as a marvelous tool to unravel the meaning of spirituality in terms of the composition of the mind. He saw it as a starting point for fulfilling his ambition to learn as much about spirituality as Newton had taught him about the physical universe. "The very thing I now want," he wrote in his diary of February 12, 1725, when he was twenty-two years old, "to give me a clearer and more immediate view of the perfections and glory of God, is as clear a knowledge of the manner of God's exerting himself, with respect to Spirits and Mind, as I have, of his operations concerning Matter and Bodies."[3] Equipped with Locke's psychology, he set for himself the task of explaining in terms of the new learning, as generations of Puritan divines had tried to do with scholastic psychology, the difference between *speculative understanding* and the sense of the heart, between an unregenerate mind and that sanctified through grace.

He attempted to use the sensationalist system to explain the traditional doctrine that "true virtue or holiness has its seat chiefly in the heart, rather than in the head. . . . The things of religion take place in men's hearts, no further than they are affected with them. The informing of the understanding is all vain, any farther than it affects the heart. . . ."[4] He endeavored to describe the regeneration of mind that occurs in conversion, and Locke's *Essay* allowed him to succeed where scholastic psychology had hampered his numerous distinguished predecessors in the Puritan tradition. But ultimately the sense of the heart could not be directly equated with anything in the Lockean lexicon. The peculiarity which had prevented an explanation of the sense of the heart by faculty psychology persisted and to some degree baffled the new sensationalism: that a feeling in the will, and not strictly speaking an idea in the understanding, constituted an apprehension. As Norman Fiering has discerned, Edwards' distinction between knowledge of the heart and speculative understanding involves "not a conative function of intellect so much as a cognitive function of the will, conceived of in the broadest possible sense, that is, where it verges into the meaning of 'heart.' "[5] The sense of the heart, as Edwards interpreted it, remains what Calvin said it was, the feeling of *suavitas,* or sweetness, in response to the promise of salvation. In Lockean psychology that could be portrayed as an actual idea of pleasure or delight. To a degree Edwards' uniqueness in the Puritan tradition was to define, apparently as the result of his own experimental knowledge of regeneration, *suavitas* as an aesthetic response and to do so as far as possible in Lockean terms.

I

As the title *An Essay Concerning Human Understanding* reveals, Locke's interests lay primarily in the cognitive power his empirical or "historical, plain method" discovered in the mind.[6] The conative power was to him relatively unimportant. In his introduction he wrote that the faculty of the understanding "sets man above the rest of sensible beings, and gives him all the advantage and dominion which he has over them."[7] It is the power to perceive in our minds ideas, or their signs, and their agreement or disagreement. So trustworthy is it, that it can construct a science of morality having the certainty of Euclidian geometry; one need only follow the methods "learned in the schools of the mathematicians, who, from very plain and easy beginnings, by gentle degrees, and a continued chain of reasonings, proceed to the discovery and demonstration of truths that appear at first sight beyond human capacity." To the will, Locke attributed no such remarkable potency, regarding it merely as the ability to consider or to forbear to consider an idea or a movement of the body (IV.iii.18; IV.xii.6–8).

Locke disclosed his conception of volition in his extensive comments on the issue of the freedom of the will. A man is free, he wrote, if he has the power to move or think "according to the preference or direction of his own mind"; liberty, in other words, pertains to the agent and not to the power he possesses (II.xxi.5–8; I.ii.6). One is free as long as one is not hindered from doing what is willed. The determiners of the agent, stated Locke, are sensations of pleasure and pain, products of the external senses and of an *internal sense*. The latter belongs to the process of reflection, whereby the mind acquires ideas by the perception of its own operations; "this source of ideas every man has wholly in himself; and though it be no sense, as having nothing to do with external objects, yet it is very like it, and might properly enough be called internal sense" (II.i.4). In response to certain ideas within the mind, feelings of pleasure or pain arise—the terms are generic and encompass delight, satisfaction, pleasure, happiness, and their opposites—and produce simple ideas. God's purpose, Locke affirmed, in having the mind join pleasurable or unpleasurable sensations to its ideas is to enable us to prefer one thought or action to another (II.vii.2–3).

Apparently Locke was not entirely happy with the results of his investigation into the freedom of the will. He admitted that originally he favored the traditional approach, namely, that the will follows the greatest good the understanding presents, but upon second thought he opted for the dictum that the greatest desire governs the will. Yet even this position, which he incorporated into the final edition of the *Essay,* required some hedging. Locke was loath to bestow upon the will, upon mere sensations of pleasure and pain, the power to determine the mind. Undercutting much of what he had written about the import of the pleasure/pain principle, he announced that reason and judgment are sovereign and can overrule the will:

> There being in us a great many uneasinesses, always soliciting and ready to determine the will, it is natural, as I have said, that the greatest and most pressing should determine the will to the next action; and so it does for the most part, but not always. For the mind having in most cases, as is evident from experience, a power to suspend the execution and satisfaction of any of its desires; and so all, one after another, is at liberty to consider the objects of them, examine them on all sides, and weigh them with others. . . . We have opportunity to examine, view, and judge of the good and evil of what we are going to do. . . . (II.xxi.48)

Locke's supposedly novel approach to the issue of the freedom of the will thus in the end reverted to the classical position that the dictate of the understanding determines the will. "Every man is put under a necessity, by his constitution as an intelligent being, to be determined in willing by his own thought and judgment what is best for him to do." The power to suspend desire makes religion the child of reason. If by chance one should be swept away by passion, then God, who surely cares about men's actions on the basis only of their highest power, reason, "who knows our frailty, pities our weakness, and requires of us no more than we are able to do, and sees what was not in our power, will judge as a kind and merciful Father" (II.xxi.54).

Immorality, Locke concluded, is error in judgment, and accordingly the remedy is to inform the understanding by means of education; one need merely "change but a man's view of these things; let him see that virtue and religion are necessary to his happiness" (II.xxi.62). Have faith in the power of reason, Locke counseled, and not only will you solve the problems of this world, but you will gain admittance into the next.

II

In his "Miscellanies" Edwards expressed his concurrence with his Puritan predecessors on the importance of the heart or inclination of the will: "The prime alteration that is made in conversion, that which is first and the foundation of all, is the alteration of the temper and disposition and spirit of the mind." To uncover the mental composition of spirituality, the changes in the mind after regeneration, he knew that he must scrutinize the will as seriously and as thoroughly as Locke had probed the understanding. In the *Enquiry,* he wrote:

> The knowledge of ourselves consists chiefly in right apprehensions concerning those chief faculties of our nature, the understanding and will. Both are very important: yet the science of the latter must be confessed to be of greatest moment; inasmuch as all virtue and religion have their seat more immediately in the will, consisting more especially in right acts and habits of this faculty.[9]

The will, to which Edwards devoted his two major works, the *Enquiry* and *Religious Affections,* he found to be virtually identical with the affections; the affections are nothing but "the more vigorous and sensible exercises of the inclination and will of the soul." The liking or disinclining of the will when presented with something to be chosen or rejected, are not, he declared, "essentially different from those affections of love and hatred."[10] In so defining the affections Edwards took Locke's less than complete theory of the passions ("desultory and superficial," his commentator Alexander Campbell Fraser calls it[11]) as the starting point for the explanation of the sense of the heart.

Committed to an exposition of the nature of the will, Edwards was generally content to let the non-conative phases of Locke's psychology stand as they had been formulated, except in one critical regard. Locke claimed that all ideas derive from observation of external objects (by means of the senses) or from the internal operations of the mind (by means of reflection). By reflecting upon the principal actions of the mind, thinking and willing, one acquires ideas of, for instance, reasoning and judging, of desiring and loving. Edwards discovered that there was a difference, which Locke failed to note, between the two sorts of ideas, those of sensation and those of reflection:

> Those ideas which we call ideas of reflection, all ideas of the acts of the mind (as the ideas of thought, of choice, love, fear, etc.)—if we diligently attend to our own minds we shall find they are not properly representations but are, indeed, repetitions of these very things, either more fully or more faintly. They, therefore, are not properly ideas. . . . And so, certainly, it is in all our spiritual ideas. They are the very same things repeated, perhaps very faintly and obscurely, and very quick and momentaneously, and with many new references, suppositions, and translations; but if the idea be perfect, it is only the same thing absolutely over again.[12]

As usual the master and not the slave of his sources, Edwards realized that ideas pertaining to mind and spirit differ from what had been described in the *Essay*. In a long entry in his "Miscellanies" labeled "Ideas, Sense of the Heart, Spiritual Knowledge or Conviction, Faith," he reported his findings; he was ready to explain the essence of the religious experience. The mind possesses two sorts of ideas. The first is representational and functions as described in the *Essay;* it serves to record a sensation, usually by means of a sign, such as a name or symbol. But the other involves an actual apprehension of the object by the repetition of the sensation that furnishes the idea; this is referred to as having a sense.

> Of things that appertain to the other faculty of the will, or what is figuratively called the heart; whereby things are pleasing or displeasing, including all agreeableness and disagreeableness, all beauty and deformity, all pleasure and pain, and all those sensations, exercises and passions of the mind that arise from either of those. An ideal apprehension or view of things of this latter sort is what is vulgarly called having a SENSE. It is commonly said when a person has an ideal view of anything of this nature, that he has a sense of it in his mind, and it is very properly so expressed. For, by what has been said already, persons can-

not have actual ideas of mental things without having those very things in the mind; and seeing all of this latter sort of mental things, that belong to the faculty of the will or the heart, do, in great part at least, consist in a sensation of agreeableness or disagreeableness, or a sense or feeling of the heart, of pleasedness or displeasedness; therefore it will follow that everyone who has an ideal view of those things has therein some measure of that inward feeling or sense.[13]

The traditional distinction between speculative knowledge and the sense of the heart, the new learning could explain, in part, as the difference between apprehension through reflection of an idea of pleasure or pain by means of a sign or through the repetition of the actual feeling. Then Edwards took a major step and expanded radically the range of ideas that were to be attributed to the sensations the will could provide:

> All that understanding of things, that does consist in, or involve, such a sense or feeling, is not merely speculative, but sensible knowledge. So is all ideal apprehension of beauty and deformity, or loveliness and hatefulness, and all ideas of delight or comfort, and pleasure of body or mind, and pain, trouble, or misery, and all ideal apprehension of desires and longings, esteem, acquiescence, hope, fear, contempt, choosing, refusing, accepting, rejecting, loving, hating, anger, and the idea of all the affections of the mind, and all their motions and exercises, and all ideal views of dignity, or excellency of any kind, and also all ideas of terrible greatness, or awful majesty, meanness or contemptibleness, value and importance. All knowledge of this sort, as it is of things that concern the heart, or the will and affections, so it all relates to the good or evil that the sensible knowledge of things this nature involves; and nothing is called a sensible knowledge upon any other account but the sense, or kind of inward tasting or feeling, of sweetness or pleasure, bitterness or pain, that is implied in it, or arises from it. (p. 137)

Locke asserted that the simple ideas of pain and pleasure usually attend sensation and reflection, that in reference to them things are considered good or evil, that they produce in us the various passions —he names love, hate, desire, joy, sorrow, hope, fear, despair, anger, and envy (*Essays*, II.xx). But Edwards, committed to the analysis of the will as the principal faculty involved in religion, decided that the sensations of pleasure and pain subsume an almost unlimited variety of ideas. They comprise a spectrum of feelings that provide the ideas that define the religious mind—ideas of beauty, loveliness, and hatefulness among others. Each is an idea of reflection, the repetition of a particular sensation. To have a sense of beauty is not simply to have an abstract idea of it, but to have the feeling of pleasure that constitutes it.

> Yet it is not only the mere ideal apprehension of that good or evil that is included in what is called being sensible; but also the ideal apprehensions of other things that appertain to the thing known, on which the goodness or evil that attends them depends. As for instance, some men are said to have a sense of the dreadfulness of God's displeasure. This apprehension of God's displeasure is called having a sense, and is to be looked upon as a part of sensible knowledge, because of the evil or pain in the object of God's displeasure, that is connected with that displeasure. But yet in a sense of the terribleness of God's displeasure there is implied an ideal apprehension of more things than merely of that pain or misery or sense of God's heart: there is implied an ideal apprehension of the being of God, as of some intellectual existence, and an ideal apprehension of his greatness and of the greatness of his power. (p. 137)

Numerous ideas of the things of religion depend upon the response of the heart. The feelings of pleasure and pain one has give an actual idea not only of good or evil but of other related qualities; to feel through a sensation of pain the evil of something may entail a feeling of dread. To feel great fear may imply a sense of the power of the being that provokes such a sensation; the more fear felt, the more power sensed.

At this point in his exposition Edwards revealed the significance he attached to his renovation of Locke's psychology. From the point of view of religion Locke's rationalism verged on triviality. The import of material existence rests with the response not of the understanding but of the will. In other contexts Edwards frequently exclaimed ecstatically over the feelings of delight, of beauty, which nature aroused; here he expressed himself objectively:

> For there is no kind of thing that we know, but what may be considered as in some respect or other concerning the wills or hearts of spiritual beings. And indeed we are concerned to know nothing on any other account; so that perhaps this distribution of the kinds of our knowledge into speculative and sensible, if duly weighed, will be found the most important of all. The distribution is with respect to those properties of

our knowledge that immediately relate to our wills and affections, and that in the objects of our knowledge on the account of which alone they are worthy to be known, viz., their relation to our wills and affections, and interest, as good or evil, important or otherwise, and the respect they bear to our happiness or misery. (p. 138)

He had probed with the newest methods of philosophy and rather than reject Calvinist piety as outmoded, discovered the profundity of its conception of spiritual knowledge; the traditional distinction between speculative and heart knowledge proved indeed to be "the most important of all." To know the good or evil, beauty or deformity of anything depends upon having a sense of the heart; without it one has merely an abstract, nearly meaningless understanding. One's spirituality in relation to everything around oneself, all of nature, heaven itself depends upon the presence of the sense of divine goodness.

To answer the question of why the spiritually endowed mind can sense goodness or moral beauty, when unregenerate it cannot, Edwards interpolated the traditional Calvinist doctrine of the inclination of the heart: the response one feels, be it pain or pleasure, good or evil, wholly depends upon the disposition of the will. A man may have an ordinary sense of beauty simply because of the laws of proportion that make something pleasing. But when it comes to spiritual matters, the will, unless grace changes its disposition, cannot respond with a sense of pleasure, or beauty, and therefore the mind cannot know what that beauty or pleasure is; it has no sense of it, but merely a word or sign of it, a representational idea.

> But the exciting sense of things pertaining to our external interest is a thing that we are so far from, and so unable to attain of ourselves, by reason of the alienation of the inclinations and natural dispositions of the soul from those things as they are; and the sinking of our intellectual power, and the great subjection of the soul in its fallen state to the external senses that a due sense of those things is never attained without immediate divine assistance. (p. 139)

Earlier in the "Miscellanies" Edwards had already made the point: the first change in the process of conversion consists of the alteration of the disposition. Grace is required before the will can feel beauty in the promise of the Gospel:

> But as to . . . a sense of divine things with respect to spiritual good and evil: because these do not consist in any agreeableness, or disagreeableness to human nature as such, or the mere human faculties, or principles; therefore men merely with the exercise of those faculties, and their own natural strength, can do nothing towards getting such a sense of divine things, but it must be wholly and entirely a work of the Spirit of God, not merely as assisting and co-working with natural principles, but as infusing something above nature. (p. 141)

After altering Locke's psychology by reformulating its theory of ideas of reflection, shaping from it a tool to plumb the will, Edwards expounded the differences between speculative and experimental knowledge with a thoroughness never permitted the old Puritan divines. His analysis complete, he preached his findings in what was to become one of his most famous sermons, "A Divine and Supernatural Light." The sense of the heart is an actual idea, a direct apprehension of goodness, of "a divine and superlative glory . . . an excellency that is of a vastly higher kind, and more sublime nature than in other things." Those who are enlightened rationally know God is good, but "he that is spiritually enlightened truly apprehends and sees it, or has a sense of it . . . has a sense of the gloriousness of God in his heart. . . . There is not only a speculatively judging that God is gracious, but a sense how amiable God is upon that account, or a sense of the beauty of this divine attribute." A speculative knowledge of good, Edwards continued, rests upon abstractions, knowing, for example, that society agrees that something furthers the common good. But the other type of knowledge involves a sense, or actual idea, "so that the heart is sensible of pleasure and delight in the presence of the idea of it. In the former is exercised merely the speculative faculty or the understanding, strictly so called, or as spoken of in distinction from the will, or disposition of the soul. In the latter, the will, or inclination, or heart, is mainly concerned." To taste the glory of God is thus to feel something, to have a certain response aroused in the will, which is the thing represented by an idea or its sign in the understanding.[14]

In emphasizing the sense of the heart as the essence of the religious experience, Edwards did not advocate an anti-intellectualism. While the sense is more important than speculative knowledge—"for a speculative without a spiritual knowledge, is to no purpose, but to make our condemnation the greater"[15]—it requires the presence of the other in order to exist. For the will to respond to a religious object, there must be a representational idea in the understanding. Only when a doctrine is first understood in this way can its excellency be felt. "A man cannot see the wonderful excellency and love of Christ in doing such and such things for sinners, unless his understanding be first informed how those things were done. He cannot have a taste of the sweetness and excellency of divine truth, unless he first have a notion that there is such a thing."[16] In order for grace to act, there must be present in the mind ideas of religion, God, and Christ, through the reading of Scripture and the instruction of the minister.[17] The more thoroughly such ideas are supplied, the more opportunity there is for grace to act. Speculative knowledge provides also what Edwards referred to as a natural sense, an ordinary response of the will, which, while not involving the Holy Spirit, can assist the supernatural sense; the natural feeling of the ugliness of evil, for example, promotes a greater sense of the glory of God's mercy.

Traditionally the difference between the devil's knowledge of spiritual things and that of the saint illustrated the wide gap between mere speculative understanding and the saving sense of the heart. Conceivably not even the greatest saint, the Puritan divine would point out from his pulpit, knew more about doctrine than the devil. But only the saint could have a sense of the doctrines. Occasionally Edwards took up the topic and shaped it to exemplify his version of the sense of the heart. Because of his great intellect, his firsthand knowledge of God's ways in governing the universe, the devil far surpasses man in knowledge, Edwards wrote in "True Grace Distinguished"; only one thing can the devil not know: "Nothing else belonging to the knowledge of God, can be devised, of which he is destitute," but he cannot have "an apprehension or sense of the supreme holy beauty and comeliness of divine things, as they are in themselves, or in their own nature."[18] The greatest deprivation the devil endures is thus his inability to feel delight in holiness, to see its spiritual beauty.

III

The sense of beauty functions as a perception. At unpredictable times the Holy Spirit engenders within the mind certain *frames* or particular dispositions which enable it to see a divine quality not only in doctrine but in the physical universe. Edwards called the quality by various names, such as *glory, holiness,* or *excellency,* but seems to have preferred the term *beauty.* He spoke from personal experience of the change in perception, as we know from his description of his own regeneration, in which he tells us that "the appearance of every thing was altered" in nature; "there seem'd to be, as it were, a calm, sweet cast, or appearance of divine glory, in almost every thing. God's excellency, his wisdom, his purity and love, seemed to appear in every thing; in the sun, moon and stars . . . and all nature."[19] Edwards frequently described the change in vision as seeming to result from a supernatural light cast on religious things, revealing their beauty or holiness. What one moment was of no great significance— perhaps a particular passage from Scripture—might the next moment be of overwhelming personal import as the light revealed its divine qualities.[20] The new perceptions of the saint originate, Edwards claimed, in the sense of the heart. Once properly disposed, the will reacts to spiritual things with a feeling of unique delight that is, as we saw above, the apprehension of beauty, beauty being psychologically a pleasurable sensation.

Sweetness is the name by which Edwards designated the unique perception, the feeling with which the regenerate will responds to the principles of religion. The term points to his continuation of the central element in the experience of faith as Calvin analyzed it, the *sensus suavitatis;* and at the same time to the Lockean psychology by which he attempted to define it; and to his preoccupation with aesthetics.

> Now this that I have been speaking, viz. the beauty of holiness is that thing in spiritual and divine things, which is perceived by this spiritual sense, that is so diverse from all that natural men perceive in them: this kind of beauty is the quality that is the immediate object of this spiritual sense: this is the sweetness that is the proper object of this spiritual taste.[21]

Just as Calvin found the *sensus suavitatis* to constitute knowledge beyond all but the saints to fathom, Edwards proclaimed that "it opens a new world to its view." It entails knowledge in several respects. First, in having the sense, the saint possesses a firsthand experience of the workings of the Holy Spirit; he enjoys, in other words, an experimental knowledge of grace, its "holy comforts and delights." Without such experience one would be, declared Edwards, "ignorant of the whole spiritual world."[22] It involves too a clearness or what Edwards sometimes referred to as a *liveliness* in one's ideas of various religious matters; after experiencing the sense the saint has, for instance, a definite or actual idea of the power of God.[23] The relations among various doctrines of religion also appear clearer. Additionally, because ideas become sharper in the mind through the operation of the sense, the saint is likely to be able to follow more easily arguments constructed on the basis of reason.[24] And, the mind may acquire new ideas, for the sense elicits new habits of devotion; they in turn, and the beauty of them, may result in further new sensations in the mind of the saint.[25]

The sense, according to Edwards, effects not only new and unique knowledge but supplies its validation as well. The feeling of sweetness in providing an actual idea of divine beauty results in the saint's having conviction; it functions as a "touchstone," "an evident stamp of divinity," "a rectified musical ear" or a "sanctified eye."[26] The beauty perceived in a doctrine is so great to the saint that he knows it to be a sign of truth, for nothing human invention can produce equals it, and therefore it must be of supernatural origin. He realizes that the sense or actual idea of beauty is what he has learned previously as mere representational idea:

> This notion of God, or idea I have of Him, is that complex idea of such power, holiness, purity, majesty, excellency, beauty, loveliness, and ten thousand other things. Now when a man is certain he sees those things, he is certain he sees that which he calls divine. He is certain he feels those things to which he annexes the term "God"; that is, he is certain that, when he sees and feels, he sees and feels. And he knows that what he thus sees and feels is the same thing he used to call God. There is such an idea of religion in his mind when he knows he sees and feels that power, that holiness, that purity, that majesty, that love, that excellency, that beauty and loveliness, that amounts to his idea of God.[27]

It follows that faith consists of the apprehension of the divine beauty in doctrines. It is conviction acquired much like an intuition, for the saint through the sense of the heart apprehends a divine quality in ideas of religion and consequently does not depend upon reason for certitude. "God and religion are the same," Edwards wrote, affirming that the saint perceives divine beauty—God—in all facets of religion; to the saint "religion is tinged with a divine color."[28] The tinge of beauty leaves no doubt in his mind of its divine origin; so he has full confidence in it. And so it is that he acquires the mercy offered in the promises of Scripture, for he sees the beauty of Christ and thus does not doubt the sufficiency of the savior to earn redemption, despite the awesome degree of sin of which the beneficiary is guilty. He can see

> the wonderful spiritual excellency of the glorious things contained in the true meaning of [the Bible], and that always were contained in it, ever since it was written; to behold the amiable and bright manifestations of the divine perfections, and of the excellency and sufficiency of Christ, and the excellency and suitableness of the way of salvation by Christ, and the spiritual glory of the precepts and promises of the Scripture.[29]

Besides enabling the saint to avoid error in his thinking, the sense of the heart permits him to choose right conduct. He knows whether a suggested action is holy or not by the presence or absence of beauty in it. False ideas about spiritual things do not harmonize with his feelings of beauty about true ideas. When a natural object is comprehended, Edwards asserted in his "Miscellanies," its various relations with other objects are perceived. This is true of spiritual things as well, because a harmony exists between one idea and another.[30] Holiness, as Edwards never tired of rehearsing, consists of spiritual harmony; God has arranged everything in proportion, and the mind upon which the Holy Spirit has bestowed the sense of the heart will reject as false that which does not harmonize with the other religious things of which it has sensible ideas.[31] Thus, for instance, it is *incongruous* that someone should have a disposition promoting feelings of sweetness in the heart over the things of religion and yet be held in disfavor by God. The saint, realizing this, feels assured of his salvation. The proposition that he is not regenerate, though he has the sense of the heart, would be inharmonious.[32] Moreover, he perceives a *perfect fitness* between Christ's excellency and the need for satisfaction of man's sin:

> The sight of this excellent congruity does very powerfully convince [the saint] of the truth of the gospel or that his way of satisfying for sin, which now they see to be so congruous. . . . The sight of this congruity convinces the more strongly, when at last it is seen, because the person

was often told of it before, yet could see nothing of it; which convinces him, that it was beyond the invention of men to discover it. . . . Now they see the perfect suitableness there is, which convinces them of the divine wisdom, totally beyond the wisdom of men, that contrived it.[33]

Once the mind perceives divine beauty, it can truly love spiritual things. The unenlightened mind finds no great pleasure in holiness because it lacks an actual idea of it, but when enabled to see divine beauty it inevitably inclines towards it. Such an inclination constitutes divine love. Occasionally, taking advantage of a simplification the old faculty psychology permitted, Edwards asserted that love follows as a consequence of the sense; the will, according to the old dictum, follows the understanding. But when he wished to describe the sense with greater precision, he identified it as itself a feeling of love, specifically a love of complacence.

> Love is commonly distinguished into a love of complacence and love of benevolence. Of these two a love of complacence is first, and is the foundation of the other,—i.e., if by a love of complacence be meant a relishing a sweetness in the qualifications of the beloved, and a being pleased and delighted in his excellency. This, in the order of nature, is before benevolence, because it is the foundation and reason of it. A person must first relish that wherein the amiableness of nature consists, before he can wish well to him on the account of that loveliness, or as being worthy to receive good.[34]

To feel sweetness in response to an object, to delight in it because of its beauty, is to have a love of complacence. The sense of the heart, it being the feeling of sweetness with which the will reacts to spiritual beauty, thus in the final analysis is a love of complacence, a love of beauty that disposes the heart benevolently.

IV

Edwards used the word *consent* to designate the new relation the mind has to God and creation after regeneration enables it to sense and to love holiness. The term signifies the harmony between the saint and what Edwards sometimes called the *system* of God, that is, the creation and providence governing it as aesthetically or harmoniously composed.

An arbiter as . . . would decide how things should proceed most fitly, according to the nature of things, would determine that the whole created system, the whole universe including all creatures animate and inanimate, should in all its proceedings or revolutions and changes, great and small, that come to pass in it, as it were, act with and from such an absolutely supreme regard to God as its last end, that every wheel both great and small of the vast machine should in all their motions move with a constant, immutable regard to God as the ultimate end, as much as if the whole system were animated and actuated by one common soul that was possessed of such perfect wisdom and rectitude.[35]

Consent, according to its etymology, means *feeling together,* harmonizing, so that Edwards without straining usage signified by it a harmonizing or agreeing *cordially,* of the heart. Once the heart or will feels love towards the system, it is in harmony with it and is part of it, according to the aesthetic principles Edwards saw governing spiritual beings. Ultimately, the sense of the heart is the perception of what Edwards called the consent to being in general; it is a glimpse of the harmony that binds the entire system of creation. It is a firsthand experience of God as the Holy Spirit, the expression of the divine harmony between the Father and the Son, perceived through the feeling of the beauty, holiness, or love (the terms are nearly interchangeable) that characterizes the system of real or substantial being.

Edwards arrived at his theory of the system of God surprisingly early in his career—it was a prominent topic of early entries in his "Notes on the Mind"—and continued to develop it in various later writings. In part he formulated it in reaction to Hobbes, as he tells us in an early note in the "Miscellanies," wanting to show that spiritual beings rather than matter are substantial. For something to be said to exist, he decided, it must be known. And therefore beings capable of knowing may be said to give existence to inanimate things. For a while Edwards toyed with idealism to support his theory of the system on an epistemological level, claiming "that the existence of the whole material universe is absolutely dependent on idea," for only an idea can be the object of the mind.[36]

But as time went on, he increasingly looked to metaphysics to explain the system of God. He took for granted various neoplatonic assumptions; he spoke, for example, of the system of creation as having a primary realm of real or substantial being, a transcendental level of existence to which ephemeral matter serves as a mere *shadow* or copy: "The glories of astronomy and natural philosophy consist in the harmony of the parts of the corporeal shadow of a world; the glories of religion consist in the sweet harmony of the greater and more-real world within themselves, with one another, and with the infinite fountain and original of them."[37] All of the realm of real being is an emanation of God's goodness, and the absence of such being is evil. "Divines are generally agreed," Edwards wrote in his *Religious Affections,* "that sin radically and fundamentally consists in what is negative, or privative, having its root and foundation in a privation or want of holiness."[38] The Cambridge Platonists may have contributed to Edwards' theory of real being, but analogues are to be found in the writing of Augustine and diverse Puritans.[39] In the *City of God,* for instance, Augustine wrote: "There is no such entity in nature as 'evil'; 'evil' is merely a name for the privation of good. There is a scale of value stretching from earthly to heavenly realities, from the visible to the invisible; and the inequality between these goods makes possible the existence of them all." Good according to Augustine constitutes a realm of transcendent being, and to lose any degree of it is to approach nothingness: "Man did not fall away to the extent of losing all being; but when he had turned towards himself his being was less real than when he adhered to him who exists in a supreme degree. And so, to abandon God and to exist in oneself, that is to please oneself, is not immediately to lose all being; but it is to come nearer to nothingness."[40] William Perkins in his famous *A Discourse of Conscience* continued in the same vein:

> Sinne properly is nothing formally subsisting, or existing (for then God should be the author of it, in as much as he is the creatour and ordainer of every thing and action,) but it is an *ataxie,* or absence of goodnesse and uprightnes, in the thing that subsisteth whereupon it is well and truly said in Schooles, *In sinne there is nothing positive,* but it is a want of that which ought to be, or subsist, partly in the nature of man, and partly in the actions of nature.[41]

Edwards gave a personal twist to the neoplatonic belief in a realm of transcendental being. He emphasized, and in this he appears to have been unique, the aesthetic nature of being. Indeed he seems to have attempted to explain in terms of aesthetics the neoplatonic conception of good as being and evil as nothingness. The basis for all aesthetic pleasure, for the feeling which responds to excellency, is in the harmony between individual objects or beings with the whole of the system of beings and with the perceiver. This is the answer he sought to one of the principal questions with which he began the notes on "The Mind": "We would know, why proportion is more excellent than disproportion; that is, why proportion is pleasant to the mind and disproportion unpleasant" (p. 21, #2). Beauty depends, he concluded, upon similarity or identity of relation between two or more objects; there can be beauty only if objects in some way are similar and have a common relation or proportion to each other or something else. An object is deformed if it does not stand in a relation similar to that of other objects. Insofar as an object is dissimilar from the rest of being, it ceases to have being and to come near to nothingness: "Disagreement or contrariety to being is evidently an approach to nothing, or a degree of nothing (which is nothing else but disagreement or contrariety of being) and the greatest and only evil; and entity is the greatest and only good. And by how much more perfect entity is, that is, without mixture of 'nothing,' by so much the more, excellency."[42] Beauty not only characterizes all existence but is vital to its nature, so much so that anything inharmonious with other things ceases to exist according to the degree of its discord. Matter and spirit, all existence, emanate from God and reflect his spiritual harmony or holiness. All harmonize according to God's design; all evince the divine love.

The harmony between spiritual beings, those possessing intelligence and will, of course cannot involve material elements. Love is the only basis for harmony among spirits:

> When we spake of excellence in bodies we were obliged to borrow the word "consent" from spiritual things. But excellence in and among spirits is, in its prime and proper sense, being's consent to being. There is no other proper consent but that of minds, even of their will; which, when it is of mind towards minds, it is love, and when of minds towards other things, it is choice. Wherefore all the primary and original beauty or excellence that is among minds is love; and into this may all be resolved that is found among them.[43]

The inclining of the will is its loving. When the will's inclination is towards the system of being, then, according to Edwards, it consents, it harmonizes by its feeling of love. This, he claimed, is what virtue really is, the cordial consent to being in general, a love which has "the great system of universal existence for its direct and immediate object."[44] All spiritual creatures and the creator are joined by the love each has for another according to the proportion of being and excellence each has. Being as God gives it forth is good; in some way Edwards never explained precisely, it is part of God, who is the sum of all entity. The more of being a creature has, the more other beings will love him. God, because he is all existence, thus receives the love of the saint.[45]

Grace is the means by which the saint acquires the sense of the heart and thus perceives the beauty of the system and harmonizes with it in love. It occasions the feeling of love towards God, "the sum of all duty," by which the saint fulfills the end for which he was created, giving glory to God.[46] Edwards described the presence of grace in the mind of the saint as an "indwelling vital principle": "The Holy Spirit operates in the minds of the godly, by uniting himself to them, and living in them, and exerting his own nature in the exercise of their faculties. . . . He acts in a way of peculiar communication of himself; so that the subject is thence denominated spiritual."[47] Grace effects in the mind something not simply "from the Spirit of God, but . . . of the nature of the Spirit of God."[48] How it is that the saint actually is in touch with God when in a gracious frame of mind, Edwards disclosed in his remarks on the Trinity.

The Holy Spirit is the love between the Father and the Son. In an "ineffable and inconceivable manner" the Spirit is a person and yet is the divine love God the Father has towards the perfect idea he has of himself, which is the Son. The Holy Spirit as the love of the Father is the inclination of the divine will; Spirit, Edwards wrote in his "Essay on the Trinity," means the "disposition, inclination or temper of the mind":

> When we read of the Spirit of God who we are told is a spirit, it is to be understood of the disposition or temper or affection of the divine mind. . . . Now the sum of God's temper or disposition is love, for He is infinite love and, as I observed before, [t]here is no distinction to be made between habit and act, between temper or disposition and exercise. This is the Divine disposition or nature that we are made partakers of, 2 Pet. i.4, for our partaking or communion with God consists in the communion or partaking of the Holy Ghost.[49]

The feeling of love, the sense of the heart, that the saint experiences when in a certain frame of mind, is God the Holy Spirit. The saint's new disposition is itself of the Holy Spirit, of the inclination of God, of God's love. So it is that the saint can experience the unique feeling of *suavitas* towards divine things. He *tastes* something of the divine love between the Father and the Son because something of it exists in him.

The love between the Father and the Son, Edwards said, is the ultimate beauty of all existence and is the source of all beauty and good. Because love is harmony between spiritual beings, the divine love between the Father and the Son is the beauty or holiness of God: " 'Tis in God's infinite love to Himself that His holiness consists. As all creature holiness is to be resolved into love, as the Scripture teaches us, so doth the holiness of God Himself consist in infinite love to Himself. God's holiness is the infinite beauty and excellency of His nature, and God's excellency consists in His love to Himself. . . ."[50] The holiness of God is his goodness as well as his beauty, and so it is that as the saint receives a new disposition of mind and harmonizes with the system, he participates in the realm of real being. He becomes part of the spectrum of good which emanates from divine love. He exists harmoniously with God, is part of the divine, aesthetic system of being.

One reason God creates is his "fulness," the term signifying for Edwards all good in God, seen as diffusing itself like a fountain of light, "as beams from the sun."[51] And since moral goodness is love, it is love for which creation provides the opportunity to expand; God creates that transcendent good and holiness might increase and be known:

> It is a thing infinitely good in itself, that God's glory should be known by a glorious society of created beings. And that there should be in them an increasing knowledge of God to all eternity, is worthy to be regarded by him, to whom it belongs to order what is fittest and best. If existence is more worthy than defect and non-entity, and if any created existence is in itself worthy to be, then knowledge is; and if any knowledge, then the most excellent sort of knowledge, viz. that of God and his glory. This knowledge is one of the highest, most real, and substantial parts of all created existence, most remote from non-entity and defect.[52]

In the feeling of divine love, the sense of the heart, the saint grasps this knowledge of God's goodness; he perceives the divine beauty of holiness, of God's love, not only as it is recorded in Scripture but as it pervades all existence. It holds the "vast machine," the system of creation, together.[53] All spiritual beings who have the Holy Spirit within them incline towards God in one grand harmony or consent consisting of an emanation of God's love. They perceive by means of the sense of the heart the harmony of divine love as it appears in other beings and is reflected in nature by the laws governing its operations and constructions—"the beauty of the body of man, and of the bodies of other animals, that sort of beauty . . . of vines, plants, trees, etc." reflects the beauty of divine love.[54] All being blossoms from the fulness of God's love and points to its source in varying degrees.

The experience of the sense of the heart is of immense importance, as Edwards views the mental dimensions of spirituality. It is the magnificent entrance to the realm of spiritual beauty, where only those of regenerate vision see the ultimate and only substantial being, the privation of which is evil. Its presence entails a qualitative difference in the mind of its possessor, a holiness of divine and beautiful love. Moral goodness is this holiness, Edwards preached, as more and more of those around him demanded a "piety" in which respectability of conduct, of doing good, of exoteric rules was to be the norm of spirituality. Steadfastly Edwards claimed "that the word 'moral' is not to be understood here [i.e., in *Religious Affections*] according to the common and vulgar acceptation of the word, when men speak of morality, and of moral behavior; meaning an outward conformity to the duties of the moral law, and especially the duties of the second table; or intending no more at farthest, than such seeming virtues, as proceed from natural principles, in opposition to those virtues that are more inward, spiritual, and divine; as the honesty, justice, generosity, good nature, and public spirit of many of the heathen, are called moral virtues, in distinction from the holy faith, love, humility, and heavenly-mindedness of true Christians. . . ."[55] Virtue is of the heart, he protested. Love of God and love of men are the same, for each is from the same source, the Holy Spirit.

Edwards used Locke's psychology to elucidate the traditional doctrine of the sense of the heart. The doctrine of the sense had presented certain problems for faculty psychology, namely, it required the will or heart to furnish perception, knowledge, and certitude, operations reserved for the understanding. Using the scheme of the *Essay* Edwards could claim that the will or heart provides the understanding with an idea of reflection. But to do justice to the Calvinist teaching on the sense, he had to refine Locke's theory of ideas and distinguish among ideas of reflection between those that are representational and those that are actual. The sense of the heart is of the latter variety; it is not a sign of a thing but the thing itself, a repetition of a feeling.

Edwards reaffirmed a traditional Calvinist teaching on the sense in describing it as a unique feeling of sweetness. But whereas Calvin and Puritan divines generally spoke of the feeling as one of gratefulness for God's mercy, Edwards, finding that moral perfection is an aesthetic quality, portrayed it as a response to divine beauty. To have the feeling of *suavitas,* he wrote, at times lyrically, is to perceive the spiritual beauty of creation and at the same time to be a part of it, to see the consent of all to God and to join in that harmony of love. The ultimate beauty of existence is that love or harmony between the Father and the Son which is the Holy Spirit; once the Holy Spirit, the divine inclination, disposes the soul of a saint righteously, there is the feeling of delight that is the sensation of holiness or divine beauty.

To some extent the contemporary scholar is predisposed to misinterpret Edwards and the Puritans. We look for philosophy in their writings, hastily pass over passages that appear to contain pietistic vagaries, and pause and ponder only when there are indications of intellectual sophistication. Yet coherent, imaginative, and influential systems of thought are often overlooked in this way. An important lexicon is ignored. Words such as *heart, relish, taste,* and *sweetness,* to name some with which these pages have been concerned, bear close scrutiny, for they often reveal products of the mind as important as any whose lineage more clearly stands respectably in the course of intellectual history.

Chapter 3
Nature, Imagination, Art—and the Earnest of What Is to Come

The Holy Spirit is the purchased possession and inheritance of the saints, as appears, because that little of it which the saints have in this world is said to be the earnest of that purchased inheritance, . . . (Eph. 1:13–14; 2 Cor. 1:22).

It pleases God a little to withdraw the veil, and let in light into the soul, and give something of a view of the great things of another world in their transcendent and infinite greatness. . . .[1]

The saint's perception, or sense, of divine beauty foreshadows his future happiness in heaven. It provides a *glimpse*, or foretaste, of what lies in store; it is a moment of ecstasy to be compounded a thousand-fold when the Holy Spirit will give all *light*, all sensation of divine holiness. The portion the saint receives of the sense in this life is the same as that which will follow "only communicated in less measure." "This vital indwelling of the Spirit in the saints," wrote Edwards, "in this less measure and small beginning, is the earnest of the Spirit, the earnest of the future inheritance. . . ." In using the term *earnest,* he recalled the federal theology, according to which the "earnest is part of the money agreed for, given in hand, as a token of the whole, to be paid in due time; a part of the promised inheritance, granted now, in token of full possession of the whole hereafter."[2] The word emphasizes that the sense of the heart, while precious, is fugitive, divine but fleeting. God ordained that the sense once felt be not permanently in the saint's possession, for if the saint can command the sense at will, there is no need for grace—he might presume to have it through his own power. Its coming and going thus remind him that his hardness of heart can be remedied only by the continued influence of Christ. Solomon Stoddard, Edwards' illustrious grandfather, explained that "if men could maintain their lively affections they would never come to Christ; therefore the Spirit of God does leave them unto, and lead them into an experimental knowledge of the hardness of their hearts."[3] Sin still remaining in the saint's heart after regeneration precludes the continuous presence of the sense; it darkens the mind, preached Edwards; "the greater the strength in which corruption is left, the more rare will be the good frames which the godly have, and the more frequent and of longer continuance will be their time of darkness."[4]

The coming and going of the sense brings the saint from ecstasy to despair, his response occasionally resembling, in modern terms, the symptoms of manic depression. Edwards' friend and student, David Brainerd, for example, described in his diary the state of his mind as consisting of periods of melancholy, marked by morbid fears of not being saved, followed by *glimpses* of divine beauty. He wrote typically: "Though I felt much dulness and want of a spirit of prayer, this week; yet I had some glimpses of the excellency of divine things; and especially one morning, in secret meditation and prayer, the excellency and beauty of holiness, as a likeness to the glorious God. . . ."[5]

Edwards himself knew well the anguish of being in a *dull* frame of mind. In the diary he kept as a young man he reported being "exceedingly dull, dry and dead" on December 21, 1722. The next day, however, he was fortunate enough to be "revived by God's Holy Spirit; affected with the sense of the excellency of holiness." A week later he noted sadly, "About sunset this day, dull and lifeless." The spiritual depression persisted into the new year. On January 2, 1723, he drew the conclusion that Puritan divines had often enumerated in their treatises on the steps to conversion; he knew, experientially, his powerlessness, knew that he himself could not control the frame of his mind. The presence of the sense, he realized *experimentally,* depends upon grace:

Wednesday, Jan. 2. Dull. I find, by experience, that, let me make Resolutions, and do what I will, with never so many inventions, it is all nothing, and to no purpose at all, without the motions of the Spirit of God. . . . I perceive, if God should withdraw his Spirit a little more, I should not hesitate to break my Resolutions, and should soon arrive at my old state. There is no dependence on myself. Our resolutions may be at the highest one day, and yet, the next day, we may be in a miserable dead condition, not at all like the same person who resolved.[6]

Much later, after extensively testing for the presence of the sense among his parishioners and carefully observing the behavior they exhibited when in gracious frames of mind, he published his findings in "A Faithful Narrative." With an objectivity and thoroughness, an empiricism, that might have pleased the Royal Society, had it been interested in evangelical religion, he wrote:

And those that have the most clear discoveries of divine truth, in the manner that has been spoken of, can't have this always in view. When the sense and relish of the divine excellency of these things fades, on a withdraw of the Spirit of God, they hadn't the medium of the conviction of their truth at command: in a dull frame they can't recall the idea, and inward sense they had, perfectly to mind; things appear very dim to what they did before; and though there still remains an habitual strong persuasion; yet not so as to exclude temptations to unbelief, and all possibility of doubting, as before: but then at particular times, by God's help, the same sense of things revives again, like fire that lay hid in ashes.[7]

The great question, given the inevitable fading of the sense, is whether it can be revived. What laws might the Holy Spirit adhere to in its work upon the mind? What can the saint do to reach or to recapture a believing frame, to stir the ashes and revive the flame? Newton-like, Edwards hoped to find a law of nature that would explain the observed comings and fadings of the sense. He noted that specific factors were sometimes present when the sense returned. For instance, talking about the sense with another, thereby recalling the experience of it, occasionally, given the presence of grace, causes its return.[8] Abigail Hutchinson, the subject of one of the two case histories contained in "A Faithful Narrative," by recounting her recent religious experiences "revived such a sense of the same things that her strength failed; and they were obliged to take her and lay her upon the bed" (pp. 194–95). A conversation about religion "served to give me a still livelier sense of the reality and excellence of divine things, and that to such a degree, as again to take away my strength, and occasion great agitation of body," his wife, Sarah, reported in the narrative documenting her reception of the sense in 1742. Her hearing accounts of religious experiences resulted in "the joy and transport of the preceding night . . . [being] renewed."9

Edwards scrupulously examined such instances of the sense's return; if the laws governing them were found, the saint might more effectively stimulate or recapture the sense. He did not assume—frequently warning that the contrary was true—that the saint has the power directly to effect within himself the sense of the heart. But, he believed, if grace is present as a holy temper or inclination of mind, then there are ways to bring on the sense. Whatever means are to be found, he realized, involve raising the affections, for of course the sense essentially is a movement of the will. In the past, evangelical preaching had worked efficaciously and consequently was "highly approved of and applauded by the generality of the people of the land, as the most excellent and profitable, and having the greatest tendency to promote the ends of the means of grace."10 Nevertheless Edwards searched for new means to occasion the sense, relying upon the psychological model of the sense of the heart he had constructed with the aid of Locke's *Essay*. He knew that the key to the problem lies in the principle that certain images in the mind can substitute for ideas of immaterial things. To raise the affections of a regenerate mind, one with a holy inclination of will, to give it a sense of divine beauty, there has to be something tangible by which a spiritual and invisible principle of religion, such as God's holiness, can be conceived. Edwards discovered that certain images are the best substitutes for spiritual phenomena; not only can they provide the mind with an actual idea to stand in place of an actual idea of spirit, but some may arouse an aesthetic feeling that can take the place of the response to, or sense of, divine beauty. An actual idea of ordinary beauty contained in an aesthetic response can stand for the sense of divine beauty. Given such images, the mind can have a natural idea of, for example, Christ's holiness, of the qualities of the divine will that are the essence of spirituality. Spiritual matters need not be so abstract as to be inconceivable, too remote to be vital. Providence ordains steps by which the mind may ascend to grasp spirit, may proceed from the sensible to the immaterial. Edwards' analysis revealed that the substitute images may derive from the mind's ideas of nature, from fantasies of the imagination, or from works of art. With such images the saint with grace in his heart may glimpse the beauty of heaven and thereby taste the earnest of heavenly joy.

I

Locke wrote in the *Essay* that if the philosopher investigates the origin of words signifying such mental phenomena as cognition and imagination, he will discover that they derive from the names of sensible things. The word *spirit,* for instance (as Emerson later echoed in *Nature*), originally meant breath, while *angel* referred to messenger. Names of spiritual objects derive from material things because the mind, to conceive of anything abstract or spiritual, requires something sensible, all knowledge ultimately stemming from sense impressions. To shape the sensationalist theory to his theological purposes, Edwards concluded that nature exists so that man can know spirit; providence ordains that the material serve the immaterial. Accordingly there is a divinely contrived correspondence between the physical and spiritual worlds. Edwards called the counterparts between spirit and matter *types,* borrowing the term from the system of Biblical exegesis wherein events in the Old Testament are interpreted as prefigurations of the coming of Christ.[11]

The creation is fraught with analogies between spirit and matter. In his notebook on *Images or Shadows of Divine Things*, Edwards spelled out his theory:

> Again it is apparent and allowed that there is a great and remarkable analogy in God's works. There is a wonderfull resemblance in the effects which God produces, and consentaneity in His manner of working in one thing and another throughout all nature. It is very observable in the visible world; therefore it is allowed that God does purposely make and order one thing to be in agreeableness and harmony with another. And if so, why should not we suppose that He makes the inferiour in imitation of the superiour, the material of the spiritual, on purpose to have a resemblance and shadow of them? We see that even in the material world, God makes one part of it strangely to agree with another, and why is it not reasonable to suppose He makes the whole as a shadow of the spiritual world?[12]

Even so insignificant a creature as the silkworm can serve as a type; it dies weaving something beautiful for man, then rises, a more glorious creature, thereby paralleling the work of redemption and the glorification of Christ.[13] And the height of heaven from the earth is analogous to the "inconceivable height of the happiness of heaven above all earthly happiness or glory."[14] The correspondences between natural facts and spiritual affairs are so precise, according to Edwards' way of thinking, that occasionally it seems God went out of his way to establish them: "I don't know but that there are some effects commonly seen in the natural world that can't be solved by any of the general laws of nature, but seem to come to pass by a particular for this very end to represent some spiritual thing, particularly that of serpents' charming of birds and squirrels into their mouths."[15]

The significance of nature, in broadest terms, consists of its analogizing the ultimate spiritual principle of divine beauty, the consent of being to being; it reflects the harmony of the wills of gracious perceiving beings to the divine will. The force of gravity, binding the matter of the universe together, is one "type of love or charity in the spiritual world,"[16] but there exists an even greater type:

> That consent, agreement, or union of being to being, which has been spoken of, viz. the union or propensity of minds to mental or spiritual existence, may be called the highest and primary beauty; being the proper and peculiar beauty of spiritual and moral beings, which are the highest and first part of the universal system, for whose sake all the rest has existence. Yet there is another, inferior, secondary beauty, which is some image of this, and which is not peculiar to spiritual beings, but is found even in inanimate things; which consists in a mutual consent and agreement of different things, in form, manner, quantity, and visible end or design; called by the various names of regularity, order, uniformity, symmetry, proportion, harmony, etc.[17]

Natural beauty—foremost the beauty of nature—typifies spiritual beauty; it mirrors the consent or harmony of the wills of perceiving beings to God. It furnishes the mind with something tangible by which spiritual or intangible beauty can be conceived. The secondary beauty is the greatest the mind is capable of apprehending without divine assistance. "We can conceive of nothing more beautiful," Edwards explained in his "Miscellanies," "of an external kind than the beauties of nature here, especially the beauty of the more animated parts of this world. We never could have conceived of these if we had not seen them; and now, we can think of nothing beyond them; and therefore the highest beauties of art consist in imitation of them."[18]

The beauty of nature, as an image, assists the mind to concep-tualize a superior beauty because it reflects the will of its creator—the source of spiritual beauty. Edwards realized relatively early in his study of the mind that any beauty, any harmony between objects, can stand for an abstract spiritual beauty, for it reflects "the appear-ance of perceiving and willing being"; for a collection of objects to stand in harmony, there has to be an arranger, an artist, a being ca-pable of knowing and willing, to order them to know of their exist-ence and to deploy them in a chosen fashion. Indeed if no mind were found to be the organizer, one would suppose, Edwards speculated, that the harmonious objects themselves possess a knowing and will-ing mind:

> The notes of a tune or the strokes of an acute penman, for instance, are placed in such exact order, having such mutual respect one to another, that they carry with them into the mind of him that sees or hears the conception of an understanding and will exerting itself in these appear-ances. And were it not that we by reflection and reasoning are led to an extrinsic intelligence and will that was the cause, it would seem to be in the notes and strokes, themselves.[19]

Art, including the greatest work of art, the creation, reflects the will of the artist, of its creator:

> Now we have shown that the Son of God created the world for this very end, to communicate Himself in an image of His own excellency. He communicates Himself, properly, only to spirits, and they only are capable of being proper images of His excellency, for they only are properly beings, as we have shown. Yet He communicates a sort of a shadow, or glimpse, of His excellencies to bodies, which, as we have shown, are but the shadows of beings, and not real beings. He, who, by His immediate influence, gives being every moment, and, by His Spirit, actuates the world, because He inclines to communicate Himself and His excellency to bodies, as far as there is any consent or analogy. And the beauty of face and sweet airs in men are not always the effect of the corresponding excellencies of mind; yet the beauties of nature are really emanations or shadows of the excellencies of the Son of God.[20]

The beauties of nature derive from Christ and consequently harmonize with spiritual beauty. The beauties of natural objects, "of the skies, trees, fields, flowers, etc." consent or harmonize with mental and spiritual beauties, and therefore are sensible communications of them; "so that, when we are delighted with flowery meadows, and gentle breezes of wind, we may consider that we see only the emanations of the sweet benevolence of Jesus Christ."[21]

Spiritual qualities in the main pertain to the will, and therefore when Edwards elaborated upon just what it is that nature reveals about Christ, he pointed not to the intellect, as those who would try to sophisticate him from the perspective of intellectual history would imply; he said nothing about secrets of a philosophic or scientific sort:

> When we behold the fragrant rose and lily, we see His love and purity. So the green trees, and fields, and singing of birds are the emanations of His infinite joy and benignity. The easiness and naturalness of trees and vines are shadows of His beauty and loveliness. The crystal rivers and murmuring streams are the footsteps of His favor, grace, and beauty. When we behold the light and brightness of the sun, the golden edges of an evening cloud, or the beauteous bow, we behold the adumbrations of His glory and goodness; and, in the blue sky, of His mildness and gentleness.[22]

To perceive through the beauties of nature the beauty of the will of Christ, to have a *sense* of its excellency, requires having certain emotional or *affectionate* experiences. In the presence of the beauty of nature, the saint's will may ascend from the feelings engendered by secondary beauty to those of spiritual beauty, may expand in its response from an ordinary sense to a sense of the heart. Henceforth nature and art have supremely important religious functions. Edwards announced what virtually amounted to being a manifesto of a new Puritan aesthetic: "the presenting of this inferior beauty, especially in those kinds of it which have the greatest resemblance of the primary beauty, as the harmony of sounds and the beauties of nature, have a tendency to assist those whose hearts are under the influence of a truly virtuous temper to dispose them to the exercises of divine love, and enliven in them a sense of spiritual beauty."[23] If the Holy Spirit has changed the inclination of the saint's will, then possibly an exposure to secondary beauty, such as that of nature, might by analogy reveal a spiritual quality; the saint might feel, as Edwards himself once felt, looking at the sky and clouds, an inexpressible "sweet sense of the glorious majesty and grace of God."[24] The appearance of everything might alter and reveal the beauty of the divine will, giving a glimpse of the earnest of what is to come.

II

Edwards voiced a popular complaint of his rationally enlightened age when he denounced the faculty of imagination as "the devil's grand lurking place, the very nest of foul and delusive spirits."[25] In his *Rambler*, the contemporaneous Samuel Johnson voiced the standard objections: "Imagination, a licentious and vagrant faculty, unsusceptible of limitations and impatient of restraint, has always endeavored to baffle the logician, to perplex the confines of distinction, and burst the inclosures of regularity."[26] In the traditional view the imagination behaved properly enough when providing images of objects actually perceived through the senses; the problem lay in its mischievous tendency to manufacture images at random and without reason, to join together diverse images, as the body of a horse and the head of a man to form the centaur—an example Hobbes cited in his *Leviathan*.[27]

Edwards, who expounded at some length the nature of the imagination, particularly in the *Religious Affections,* followed the classical schema, defining it as the power to have an idea of an external object when it was not present to the senses. From the theological point of view, he explained, the danger lies in the imagination's abetting enthusiasm, that is, "all the imaginary sights of God and Christ and heaven, all supposed witnessing of the Spirit, and testimonies of the love of God by immediate inward suggestion."[28] At times an overly zealous person, the likes of Anne Hutchinson, might imagine a voice reciting passages from Scripture or delivering a personal admonition, or might see a great shining light and believe such fantasies to be personal revelations from God. By such means the imagination brews extraordinary fanaticism, spawns false religions, wantonly raises the affections, and thereby hinders the progress of true evangelical piety.[29] Thus can the imagination be the devil's lurking place. In pointing out the danger Edwards adhered to the enlightened standards of his own age and to the orthodox position of the Puritanism of the previous century. Indeed, to elaborate further upon the warning, he quoted freely from various seventeenth-century Puritan authorities, Anthony Burgess, François Turretine, Thomas Shepard, John Smith, and John Flavel, who, in a vein pursued with equal vehemence by the others, complained that "conceits and whimseys abound most in men of weak reason; children, and such as are cracked in their understanding have most of them; strength of reason banishes them, as the sun does mists and vapors."[30] Underscoring the traditional warning, Edwards argued that the legitimate emotions of the religious experience arise not from the visions of the imagination but from true spiritual light.

But though firmly supporting the accepted standard and emphatically denying that visions contributed by the imagination can be the efficient cause of religious affections, Edwards nevertheless bespoke an important place for the faculty. First he noted that the presence of imaginary phenomena does not of itself signal false affections. "Before I finish what I would say on this head of imaginations, counterfeiting spiritual light, and affections arising from them, I would renewedly (to prevent misunderstanding of what has been said) desire it may be observed, that I am far from determining that no affections are spiritual which are attended with imaginary ideas."[31] Cautiously Edwards disclosed that the imagination might indeed serve an important psychological function in the experience of the sense of the heart by *attending* it. Edwards announced that imaginings, even visions, often accompany the sense. The imagination in fact is at times vital to the occurrence of the religious experience: "Such is the nature of man, that he can scarcely think of any thing intensely, without some kind of outward ideas. They arise and interpose themselves unavoidably, in the course of a man's thoughts; though oftentimes they are very confused, and are not what the mind regards."[32] More importantly, the imagination can invent images, "outward ideas," so that ideas of spiritual things can be conceived. In "The Distinguishing Marks" Edwards boldly declared that the imagination is positively necessary to acquire knowledge of spirit:

> Such is our nature that we can't think of things invisible, without a degree of imagination. I dare appeal to any man, of the greatest powers of mind, whether or no he is able to fix his thoughts on God or Christ,

or the things of another world, without imaginary ideas attending h meditations?

> As God has given us such a faculty as the imagination, and has so made us that we can't think of things spiritual and invisible, without some exercise of this faculty, so it appears to me that such is our state and nature, that this faculty is really subservient and helpful to the other faculties of the mind, when a proper use is made of it; though oftentimes when the imagination is too strong, and the other faculties weak, it overbears 'em, and much disturbs them in their exercise. It appears to me manifest in many instances I have been acquainted with, that God has really made use of his faculty to truly divine purposes. . . .[33]

Going yet a step further, and seemingly parting company with traditional Puritan teaching, he defended the most controversial products of the imagination, visions. Like objects from nature, they permit the mind to conceive of spirit, though in themselves, Edwards emphasized, they are not spiritual; they accompany the sense of the heart, but are not the origin of it.[34] When the saints experience the sense of the heart, they may very well have visions in order better to conceive divine beauty; they may reach a feeling of "ecstasy, wherein they have been carried beyond themselves, and have had their minds transported into a train of strong and pleasing imaginations, and kind of visions, as though they were wrapped up even to heaven, and there saw glorious sights."[35]

Edwards built his theory of the religious function of the imagination upon a foundation of empirical evidence. Abigail Hutchinson, for instance, told him of having for several days at a stretch "a constant ravishing view of the glory of God and Christ," "a kind of beatific vision of God."[36] His wife, Sarah, reported that while in a gracious frame of mind she had seen those known to her to be awakened surrounded by the glory which would be theirs in heaven: "When I saw them, my heart went out towards them, with an inexpressible endearedness and sweetness. I beheld them by faith in their risen and glorified state, with spiritual bodies re-fashioned after the image of Christ's glorious body, and arrayed in the beauty of heaven. The time when they would be so, appeared very near, and by faith it seemed as if it were present."[37] In the account of his own conversion, the "Personal Narrative," Edwards noted that while tasting the "inward sweetness" of the sense, he experienced "a kind of vision, or fix'd ideas and imaginations, of being alone in the mountains, or some solitary wilderness, far from all mankind, sweetly conversing with Christ, and wrapt and swallowed up in God."[38] Because of the harmony between natural beauty and that of spirit, he wrote in "Excellency of Christ," it is natural in a gracious frame of mind to think of the beauties of natural phenomena, skies, trees, and flowers, "and [to] fancy ourselves in the midst of them."[39]

Deistic, rationalist approaches made religion, Edwards claimed, a "mere formality," the mere "regulating of men's lives according to the rules of virtue and piety."[40] Hobbes had argued the case long before; man can properly conceive only of the finite, the sensible, and therefore he can have no real or empirical knowledge of divinity:

> No man can have in his mind an image of infinite magnitude; nor conceive infinite swiftness, infinite time, or infinite force, or infinite power. When we say any thing is infinite, we signify only, that we are not able to conceive the ends, and bounds of the things named; having no conception of the thing, but of our own inability. And therefore the name of God is used, not to make us conceive him, for he is incomprehensible; and his greatness, and power are unconceivable; but that we may honour him. Also because, whatsoever, as I said before, we conceive, has been perceived first by sense, either all at once, or by parts; a man can have no thought, representing any thing, not subject to sense.[41]

In his "Notes on Natural Science," an unpublished notebook, Edwards addressed the issue directly as it pertained to physics, asking how the mind can conceive of what cannot be sensed. In answer he wrote of the "prejudice of the imagination," by which he meant not to attack the imagination *per se*, as the article generally seems to be interpreted as signifying, but to underscore the danger of inflexibility of imagination. The extent to which a man's power of imagination is limited, the less capacity he has to conceive validly of phenomena not sensible: the wonders of the Newtonian universe—and of God's creation. "And truly," he wrote, "I hardly know of any other prejudices, that are more powerful against truth of any kind, than those." Set ways of imagining "are beat into us by every act of sensation . . . [and] it is almost impossible to root them out." Men measure by what they can perceive with their senses; and this is the great prejudice of the imagination, "so that there must be no body, forsooth, bigger than they can conceive of, or less than they can see with their eyes: no motion, either much swifter, or slower, than they can imagine." Every man should be "clean out of conceit with his imagination" because if his power of imagining is not free of the parameters of sense knowledge, he cannot have a true conception of the universe and its immense distances. An inspired young Edwards then ventured further to prove his point by advancing two propositions that tax the mind's imaginative powers but that are nevertheless true: "there is no degree of swiftness of motion whatever, but what is possible"; secondly, "there may be bodies of any infinite degree of smallness."[42] In turning to the imagination so that the mechanical Newtonian universe could be validly conceived, the extraordinarily sophisticated young Edwards reached a new epistemological perspective, which he planned to present in the proposed treatise on the mind, where he would examine "how far imagination is unavoidable in all thinking and why."[43] In discovering the importance of the imagination Edwards joined a movement which, according to Livingston Welch, eventually would lead to romanticism: the mathematically ordered seventeenth-century Cartesian world, analyzable by reason, was beginning to be replaced by the Newtonian world, held together not by logical relations, but by material particles bound temporally and spatially, analyzable only by dependence upon the imaginative power to view the particles as combined into a whole.[44]

Besides providing images by which non-material beings and principles could be conceived, the imagination, Edwards concluded, benefited the mind spiritually in another respect. Ideas of spirit are ideas of reflection, those which derive from the mind's own responses rather than from external stimuli; as Edwards interpreted and expanded the psychology of Locke, spirituality primarily is a matter of the will, an affection, a particular feeling of love, a unique response to divine beauty—generically a feeling of pleasure or pain, if strictly classified according to the *Essay*. The will's reaction to beauty functions as an apprehension of that beauty, a sense of it, just as to feel terror in "God's displeasure there is implied an ideal apprehension of the being of God, as of some intellectual existence, and an ideal apprehension of his greatness and of the greatness of his power."[45] By means of the imagination the mind can receive a natural idea of spirit; by the images it presents, the imagination can excite in the mind feelings that resemble spiritual feelings and that can therefore substitute for them in thinking. The mind cannot have an actual reflective idea, or sense, of divine beauty without grace; but if the mind imagines or projects itself into circumstances that excite a sense of love or beauty, then it may acquire a tangible (*sensible*) idea by which to represent what otherwise is beyond it.

> When we have the idea of another's love to a thing, if it be the love of a man to a woman that we are unconcerned about, we neither love in such cases nor have generally any proper idea at all of his love. We only have an idea of his actions that are the effects of love, as we have found by experience, and of those external things which belong to love and which appear in case of love. Or if we have any idea of it, it is either by forming our ideas so of persons and things, as we suppose they appear to them, that we have a faint vanishing notion of that affection; or if the thing be a thing that we so hate that this can't be, we have our love to something else faintly, at least, excited, and so in the mind, as it were, referred to that place. We think this is like that.[46]

By imagining two lovers, or by recalling the feeling of love one has had, imagination and memory at times being virtually identical, the mind has a tangible representation of a spiritual feeling. Once freed of its "prejudices," the imagination empowers the mind to conceive that "the Fixed Stars can be so distant as that the Earth's annual revolution should cause no parallax among them," and also permits the conceptualization of spirit.[47] Empiricism need not reduce religion to abstractions, to mere ethical norms, to what in the long history of reformed thought has been termed *speculative* rather than *heart* knowledge. The imagination can make the things of religion seem vital rather than remote. Through the imagination the sinner may have a vivid picture of hell, may have "lively ideas of a dreadful furnace,"[48] and thereby feel great fear and acquire an idea of God's dreadfulness; or he may imagine the beauty of a setting in nature and receive an idea resembling that of a taste of divine beauty. The images, such as that of the sun as a representation of God the Father, rarely will be new—they usually are suggested by the figurative language of the Bible—but they allow the mind to grasp spirit.[49] The imagination enables the saint to come as close as is possible, without the intervention of grace, to a glimpse, an *earnest,* of divine beauty. By imagining great natural beauty and the aesthetic feeling it instills, the saint stands in a better position to receive the actual earnest of divine beauty.

III

Occasionally Edwards' attitude toward art has seemed less than en-
thusiastic. Dwight found the remarks on style in the preface to "Five
Discourses" to be disappointingly indifferent; here was an avowal of
a definite disdain of "such ornaments as politeness and modishness
of style and method." Edwards unabashedly averred, "However un-
able I am to preach or write politely, if I would, yet I have this to com-
fort me under such a defect, that God has shewed us he does not need
such talents in men to carry on his own work, and that he has been
pleased to smile upon and bless a very plain unfashionable way of
preaching."[50] Yet the distaste early in his career for *polished* writing,
an echo of the disapproval of *human invention* in religious matters
long espoused by Puritan advocates of the plain style, his inattention
to the state of manuscripts submitted for publication, and his neglect
to treat fully the place of art in his aesthetic view of the creation do
not mean that he held art to be inconsequential theologically. Scat-
tered through his writings are remarks, often made in passing and
nowhere thoroughly developed, that suggest the importance he attached to art as a means to receive or to revive the sense of the heart.

Edwards appears to have commented more often on music than
any other art, perhaps because singing had been a staple of Puritan
worship, while icons decidely had not been. Given his aesthetic bent,
his interpretation of the religious experience as being the apprehension of divine beauty, it is hardly surprising that he directed particular attention to one of the few art forms to be found commonly in
provincial New England. Singing was at hand, was an accepted form
of worship. He summarized its importance with: "Music, especially
sacred music, has a powerful efficacy to soften the heart into tender-
ness, to harmonize the affections, and to give the mind a relish for objects of a superiour character."[51] Music stood, he realized, quite
clearly in analogy with spirit. Its tonal harmonies represent the con-
senting of wills that composes God's realm of sanctified beings.
"When one thing," he wrote, "sweetly harmonizes with another, as
the notes in music, the notes are so conformed and have such propor-
tions one to another that they seem to have respect one to another as
if they loved one another."[52] Thus music may serve, along with
images culled from nature or created by the imagination, to aid in the

conceptualization of spirit; it provides something sensible to aid in the conceiving of spirit. The harmony of music may seem to the mind in a gracious frame to be like the spiritual consent between God and the beings whose wills incline to him. Because of its resemblance to consent between spiritual beings, it expresses almost ideally the love among the saints; the system in heaven by which they converse presumably will be, Edwards speculated in several entries of the "Miscellanies," a superior sort of music.[53]

Art has a vital religious function. The discovery, perhaps Edwards' most significant contribution to the Puritan tradition in American letters, he based on the principle that natural beauty possesses "a tendency to assist those whose hearts are under the influence of a truly virtuous temper to dispose them to the exercises of divine love, and enliven in them a sense of spiritual beauty."[54] Though Edwards did not pursue and explain the point as fully as we might wish, the outlines of his theory of the spiritual efficacy of art are clear. Art can elicit emotion, call forth an aesthetic response, that resembles the religious response to divine beauty. The essence of religion or spirituality, "that inward sensation, or kind of spiritual sense, or feeling, and motion of the soul, is what is called affection";[55] therefore to raise the affections most similar to the sense brings the mind as near to the real thing as it can go without divine assistance. Thus Edwards announced: "The duty of singing praises to God, seems to be appointed wholly to excite and express religious affections. No other reason can be assigned, why we should express ourselves to God in verse, rather than in prose, and do it with music, but only, that such is our nature and frame, that these things have a tendency to move our affections."[56] The role Edwards assigned to art constitutes a substantial evolution from that present in the aesthetics of such Puritans as Richard Baxter.[57] Art in raising the affections that most resemble the sense of the heart may prompt a response to primary, or spiritual, beauty, or at least may provide an idea of it. This is not to say that Edwards fully developed the place of art in his aesthetic system. But the import of art in his scheme appears often in his writings, particularly in *The Nature of True Virtue* and in the "Miscellanies."

Edwards singled out hymnal verse as a means to excite religious affections, apparently at least in part as the result of empirical observation. Hymn lyrics, for instance, played a prominent part in the occurrences of the sense his wife reported in her written account of

religious experience. Several times Sarah referred to the effects produced by reciting or recalling the inspirational lyrics of such popular
evangelical versifiers as Ralph Erskine (1685–1752), Mrs. Elizabeth
Singer Rowe (1721–1803), and Isaac Watts (1674–1748).[58] During
one interval of intense pietistic verve, some lines of Watts came to her
mind. "I uttered them," she wrote, "as the real language of my heart.
. . . And while I was uttering the words, my mind was so deeply impressed with the love of Christ, and a sense of his immediate presence, that I could with difficulty refrain from rising from my seat,
and leaping for joy. I continued to enjoy this intense, and lively and
refreshing sense of Divine things, accompanied with strong emotions, for nearly an hour. . . ." Hearing someone read "a melting
hymn of Dr. Watts, concerning the loveliness of Christ, the enjoy-
ments and employments of heaven, and the Christian's earnest desire
of heavenly things . . . I leaped unconsciously from my chair. I seemed
to be drawn upwards, soul and body, from the earth towards Christ
and heaven; and it appeared to me that I must naturally and necessarily ascend thither."[59] The most exhilarating moment resulted
from her recalling these lines of Mrs. Rowe:

> More I would speak, but all my words are faint:
> Celestial Love, what eloquence can paint?
> No more, by mortal words, can be expressed;
> But vast eternity shall tell the rest.

The words left her feeling faint for some time, but soon after recol-
lecting them she "had a still more lively and joyful sense of the goodness and all-sufficiency of God."[60]

Edwards' own response to religious verse, while apparently no less
fervid, was more discriminating than Sarah's, his interest more creative. Though he was familiar with a number of poets—including
Sarah's favorites, Watts and Rowe, and several now thought more
deserving, such as Milton, Pope, and Edward Young[61]—he reserved
his most telling observations about poetry for certain lyrical passages
from the Bible. In an entry made in the "Miscellanies" he wrote that
the Psalms and certain other parts of Scripture possess extraordinarily beautiful images as the result of poetic inspiration and the
influx of grace combined:

> The fire of grace together with a true poetical genius naturally guided
> them [the writers of Scripture] to make use of such images as almost lit-

erally described the affairs of the Gospel of which all in the Jewish Church was a shadow and representation, the most natural that could be, and representations so natural that a poetical genius so exalted and animated by lively and vigorous grace would by them be naturally led to the ideas of Gospel things.[62]

Nature offers the poet images that by divine contrivance, that by analogy, represent spirit and so are the best, the most natural means to represent spiritual matters; "for there is a most wonderful analogy and natural correspondence between one and the other which one will see the more, the more they have of a poetical and gracious disposition, and clear and comprehensive understanding of those matters."[63] Figurative language is vital to the representation of religious subjects. Its purpose is not merely to entice and to arouse spiritually dull minds by appeal to the senses; it is the ordained or natural means of expression of spirit. Metaphor derives from the images of nature, and therefore it expresses the *airs* that correspond to divine spiritual qualities: just as the countenance of someone might suggest graceful airs, spiritual excellencies of mind, "there is really likewise an analogy or consent between the beauty of the skies, trees, fields, flowers, etc., and spiritual excellencies. . . . Those have their airs, too, as well as the body and countenance of man." The objects of nature, and therefore the metaphors founded upon them, communicate spiritual qualities, namely the will of God. Flowers signify love, trees give an idea of rejoicing, and thunder reflects the majesty of God.[64] The true poet perceives the analogy between matter and spirit and consequently can mine nature for the divinely contrived metaphors. He perceives in nature the attributes of the divine will: love, mercy, majesty, spiritual beauty.

In the "Personal Narrative," Edwards described his own response to the lyrical passages of Scripture that had been instrumental in his conversion. His first experience of the sense of the heart occurred when reading "Now unto the King eternal, immortal, invisible, the only wise God, be honor and glory for ever and ever, Amen" (1 Tim. 1:17). As he read these words, he tells us, "there came into my soul, and was as it were diffused thro' it, a sense of the glory of the Divine Being; a new sense, quite different from any thing I ever experienced before." He began to sing the words to himself, prayed in a manner different from what he used to, and acquired "a new kind of apprehensions and ideas of Christ." He notes also that "I am the Rose of Sharon, the lily of the valleys" had a special significance for him, the words representing the beauty of Christ.

But the clearest sign of the extent to which he associated the sense with lyricism appears in what he tells us next. Finding that "the appearance of every thing was altered," that he could perceive the beauty of God's will in nature—"his purity and love, seemed to appear in everything; in the grass, flowers" etc.—he notes that he began "singing forth with a low voice, my contemplations of the Creator and Redeemer." Lyricism he found to be the natural means to express the sense of the heart. Thunder used to terrify him, but he came to hear God's majesty in it; hearing it would lead to contemplation of God: "and while I viewed, used to spend my time, as it always seem'd natural to me, to sing or chant forth my meditations; to speak my thoughts in soliloquies, and speak with a singing voice." His extemporaneous versifying continued. Year after year, he tells us, he would walk alone in the woods "and it was always my manner, at such times, to sing forth my contemplations."[65]

Edwards' involvement with religion, as the attentive reader of his "Miscellanies" and notebooks comes to know, was passionate; he was an emotional man, though he lived in an age infatuated with reason and though he thought and argued with marvelous clarity and invincible logic. Singing in church or, when alone in the woods, chanting his praise of the ineffably beautiful creation he perceived, Edwards naturally took to an aesthetically pleasing means of expression. He would "speak with a singing voice." Unfortunately little survives of Edwards' lyrical outpourings; he did set down, at the beginning of the "Miscellanies," the beautiful short piece "Of holiness," in which, using images taken from nature, he tried to express that holiness "made the soul like a field or garden of God, with all manner of pleasant flowers."[66] Most famous of his lyrical writing, of course, is the prose poem thought to be about Sarah, which Perry Miller has called an apostrophe, a hymn, and a love lyric.[67] And there is the "Excellency of Christ." But delightful as these pieces are, they hardly realize the potential of the aesthetic Edwards constructed. The student of Edwards consequently faces the question, probably never to be entirely answered, of why he did not more fully exploit his theory of the office nature, imagination, and art perform in calling forth the sense of the heart. Perhaps, in some measure, he was too absorbed in tract wars to pay sufficient attention to his non-polemic writings.[68] Ironically Edwards may in the end have proved to be the victim of his own finely honed philosophic arguments, the time and labor spent in their composition being taken away from exercises more pleasing to prosperity. It remained for Emerson to fructify and harvest what Edwards had sown, to develop and expand the theory of the religious function of nature, the imagination, and art.

Chapter 4
Lively Pictures, the Use of Art

I do not suppose that they themselves imagined that they saw anything with their bodily eyes; but only have had within them ideas strongly impressed, and as it were, lively pictures in their minds: as for instance, some when in great terrors, through fear of hell, have had lively ideas of a dreadful furnace. Some, when their hearts have been strongly impressed, and their affections greatly moved with a sense of the beauty and excellency of Christ, it has wrought on their imaginations so, that together with a sense of his glorious spiritual perfections, there has arisen in the mind an idea of one of glorious majesty, and of a sweet and a gracious aspect.[1]

The imagination, Edwards believed, may advance evangelical religion in another way besides conjuring up ordinary ideas and feelings to substitute for those involving spirit. It can enable the mind to grasp circumstances never actually experienced; one may imagine, or be led to imagine, being perched precariously over a pit, then sliding helplessly and frantically into the bowels of hell. The imagination permits conceptualization of what cannot be sensed, the horrors of eternal damnation being a foremost instance. If one does not have a convincing idea of the terror which the unconverted are doomed to feel, a real feeling of anguish, one will not turn to Christ and beg for mercy. Thus to an extent one's spiritual fate may hinge upon the ability to imagine the awful punishment of hell. Much of what Scripture reports of the past and foretells of the future, Edwards realized, the imagination alone can make seem real to the mind, dependent as it is, from the Lockean perspective, upon sense knowledge. If the Bible is to be believed with conviction, if the mind is truly to grasp the revelations about heaven and hell, then there must be something tangible for conceptualization, and that the imagination may provide. Edwards in time came to view the imagination not merely as a means to ornament truth, as had been traditionally taught, but as a means to arrive at it. The epistemological principle he discovered is that

> A man may have a sensible apprehension of pleasure, or sorrow [the ideas that comprise our sense of spiritual matters], that others are the subjects of, indirectly by reflection; either by exciting from the memory something that he has felt heretofore, which he supposes is like it, or by placing himself in others' circumstances, or by placing things about him in his imagination, and from ideas so put together in his mind, exciting something of a like pleasure or pain transiently in himself. Of [*sic;* or] if those ideas come so together into the mind by the senses, or by the relation of others, such a sensation will spontaneously arise in the mind. In like manner, men may have a sense of their own happiness or misery conceived as future. So men may, by mere nature, come to have a sense of the importance, or terribleness, or desirableness of many things.[2]

Managed properly by the evangelical preacher, the imagination, Edwards discovered, contributes discursively and at the same time artistically to his sermon; using the props of art to construct a fictive situation, he can convey a sense of the horrors of hell or of the beauty of sanctity.

I

Calvin claimed that religious icons and paintings lead at worst to idolatry, at best to a debasement of divine glory. "All we conceive concerning God in our minds is an insipid fiction," for the essence of God is incomprehensible, and so artistic images cannot represent him; they but signify man's effort to reduce the unknowable to the level of human comprehension.[3] In the *Institutes* Calvin stated the position towards art in religion that would, generally, set the parameters adopted by the Puritans:

> And yet I am not gripped by the superstition of thinking absolutely no images permissible. But because sculpture and paintings are gifts of God, I seek a pure and legitimate use of each, lest those things which the Lord has conferred upon us for his glory and our good be not only polluted by perverse misuse but also turned to our distraction. We believe

it wrong that God should be represented by a visible appearance, because he himself has forbidden it (Ex. 20:4) and it cannot be done without some defacing of his glory. . . . If it is not right to represent God by a physical likeness, much less will be allowed to worship it as God, or God in it. Therefore it remains that only those things are to be sculptured or painted which the eyes are capable of seeing: let not God's majesty, which is far above the perception of the eyes, be debased through unseemly representations. (1.xi.12)

Calvin scoffed at the claim that images were necessary to assist the uneducated, insisting that all one need be taught is that Christ through his death expiated our sins. Though his position left some room for the employment of images in religion, he implied clearly that the risk was great, the benefit minimal. Among the Puritans, John Cotton explicitly excluded images, vigorously maintaining the conception of the transcendent, incomprehensible God: "It matters not whether the Image be a thing truly existent, formed of any visible matter, Brass, Wood, or Stone; or whether it have no other being but in the mind of men. If it be an Image devised by men for Religious use, it commeth under the sentence of the Law. . . ."[4] Thus even mental pictures were condemned.

Recent scholarship has shown that despite such expressions of iconophobia, Puritans quite often—especially in poetry, sermons, and tombstone carvings—resorted to images of heaven and hell, even of Christ and of God.[5] The justification or rationalization for such practice has not been easy to discern, the Puritans having no fully stated *ars poetica*. Robert Daly suggests that they distinguished between images of God and those taken from the sensible world, and shunned only the former, an approach which would fall within the letter if not the spirit of Calvin's teaching (p. 48).

Puritan validation of images appears mainly in a small body of commentary on meditation, most extensively in Richard Baxter's influential, frequently reprinted *The Saints Everlasting Rest* (1650), in which Daly finds "the theological rationale for the figures that constitute so much of Puritan religious poetry . . . , the explicit statement of the attitude that enabled Puritan poets to delight in the sensible world . . ." (p. 79). Baxter discloses the function, from a Puritan point of view, of the imagination in raising the sense of the heart, the feeling of sweetness, or *suavitas*. The imagination, he explains, can help "to make your Meditations of Heaven more quickening, and to make you taste the sweetness that is therein . . . that you may not stick in a bare thinking, but may have the lively sense of all upon your hearts."[6] Baxter's discussion, instrumental in formulating a Puritan aesthetic, markedly contrasts with the position Edwards arrived at almost a century later, after reading Newton and Locke.[7]

The mind, according to Baxter, can properly conceive of only what the senses can perceive, and therefore faith presents a problem, for "it is no easie matter to rejoyce at that which we never saw, nor ever knew the man that did see it." But indirectly the senses can aid the mind to acquire an idea of spirit: "God would not have given us, either our Senses themselves, or their usual objects, if they might not have been serviceable to his own praise, and help to raise us up to the apprehension of higher things." To permit the mind to grasp spiritual things, the Holy Spirit represents them "in words that are borrowed from the objects of Sense. . . . He describeth the glory of the New Jerusalem, in expressions that might take even with flesh itself: As that the Streets and Buildings are pure Gold, that the Gates are Pearl, that a Throne doth stand in the midst of it, &c." Figurative language, based as it is upon objects of sense, enables the mind to substitute easily conceivable objects for those that cannot be sensed, and accordingly its use is sanctioned by Scripture: "if such expressions had not been best, and to us necessary, the Holy Ghost would not have so frequently used them: He that will speak to mans understanding, must speak in mans language, and speak that which he is capable to conceive." The imagination, by the same principle, also is permitted as a necessary means to conceive of the immaterial; it allows us to place objects of sense in the stead of spirit. Baxter encourages its use within moderation:

> Draw as strong suppositions [i.e., imaginations] as may be from thy sense for the helping of thy affections. It is lawful to suppose [i.e., imagine] we did see for the present, that which God hath in Prophecies revealed, and which we must really see in more unspeakable brightness before long. Suppose therefore with thy self thou hadst been that Apostles fellow-traveller into the Celestial Kingdom, and that thou hadst seen all the Saints in their White Robes, with Palms in their hands. Suppose thou hadst heard those Songs of Moses, and of the Lamb; or didst even now hear them praising and glorifying the Living God. If thou hadst seen these things indeed, in what a rapture wouldst thou have been? And the more seriously thou puttest this supposition to thy

self, the more will the Meditation elevate thy heart. I would not have thee, as the Papists, draw them in Pictures, nor use mysterious, significant Ceremonies to represent them. This, as it is a course forbidden by God, so it would but seduce and draw down thy heart. But get the *liveliest Picture* of them in thy minde that possibly thou canst; meditate of them; till thou canst say, Methinks I see a glympse of the Glory! methinks I hear the shouts of joy and praise![8]

Something of the same benefit accrues to the understanding when the Puritan divine employs the imagination to manufacture figurative expressions, such as similitudes, and thereby equips his sermons with a diction of the concrete. But Baxter warns that images must not "seduce and draw down the heart"; if used improperly, they may attract the mind's attention to themselves. The aesthetic Baxter sketched, in the final analysis, maintains that images are useful and necessary devices but are not identifiable with or inseparable from that which they serve to illustrate:

But what is my scope in all this? is it that we might think Heaven to be made of Gold and Pearl? or that we should Picture Christ as the Papists do, in such a shape? or that we should think Saints and Angels do indeed eat and drink? No; Not that we should take the Spirits figurative expressions, to be meant according to strict propriety; or have fleshly conceivings of Spiritual things, so as to beleeve them to be such indeed. But thus: To think that to conceive or speak of them in strict propriety, is utterly beyond our reach and capacity; and therefore, we must conceive of them as we are able; and that the Spirit would not have represented them in these notions to us, but that we have no better notions to apprehend them by; and therefore that we make use of these phrases of the Spirit to quicken our apprehensions and affections, but not to pervert them. . . .

Baxter thus regards figurative language ambivalently; it is necessary so that the mind can conceptualize what is immaterial, yet it distorts what it represents; "these phrases though useful, are but borrowed and improper" (pp. 758–59), for, after all, Heaven really does not have streets of gold and pearl. The Puritan aesthetic, as Perry Miller has shown, separates content from form; figurative expression does not stand intrinsically connected to the truth it represents.[9]

Besides being an aid to conceptualization, the tropes of the imagination serve another purpose. As Michael Wigglesworth claimed, in *The Prayse of Eloquence* (1650), "by the power of eloquence ould truth receivs a new habit; though its essence be the same yet its visage is so altered that it may currently pass and be accepted as a novelty. The same verity is again and again perhaps set before the same guests but drest and disht up after a new manner."[10] The Puritan divine following such a scheme exercised his creative powers to turn up similes and metaphors so that the understanding perceived a given truth in a new light, while the affections were caught by the delightful surprise the trope presented. To foster such surprise, he resorted to an array of similitudes, often of a homely, or familiar, character. Thomas Hooker, for example, urged that everyone watch his heart to free it of impurities: "you may conceive it by a similitude, if a pot be boyling upon the fire, there will a scum arise, but yet they that are good housewives, and cleanly, and neat, they watch it, and the scum riseth up, they take it off and throw it away, happily more scum will arise, but still as it riseth they scum it off."[11]

To force home the "ould truth" that unless the sinner repents and turns to Christ for mercy he will burn in hell forever, generations of Puritan ministers employed numerous similitudes to suggest the degree of pain that would be endured in hell, the righteous anger of the omnipotent God, and the despair the damned would feel in their realization that their sufferings would never end because they had neglected in life the means to grace.[12] To help the congregation to some sensible idea of the extent of pain the fires of hell would inflict, the minister might suggest that they measure from the hurt felt under ordinary circumstances. "O consider of this wrath before you feel it," wrote Thomas Shepard; "Thou canst not endure the torments of a little kitchen-fire, on the tip of thy finger, not one half hour together. How wilt thou bear the fury of this infinite, endless, consuming fire, in body and soul throughout all eternity. . . ?"[13] The congregation might be asked to consider the divine wrath by comparing it to the torments of human invention: "A man may devise exquisite torments for another, and great power may make a little stick to lay on heavy strokes; but great power stirred up to strike from great fury and wrath makes the stroke deadly. I tell thee, all the wisdom of God shall then be set against thee to devise torments for thee."[14]

From Edwards' point of view, the traditional Puritan aesthetic accomplished but at the same time undermined its purpose. While its panoply of similes enlivened old truths, capturing the affections by the unexpected aptness of the trope, it failed to instill the sort of ror that constituted an actual idea of hell—which might result i figurative expression were more closely identified with what it ᴿᵉᵖ- resents. The point can be illustrated by a passage written by Thomas Shepard, whom Edwards thought so highly of as to cite more than any other authority in the *Religious Affections;* it may be the origin of the image in "Sinners in the Hands of an Angry God" of the sinner hanging by a thread, ready to drop into hell:

> They [i.e., sinners] are ready every moment to drop into hell. God is a consuming fire against thee, and there is but one paper wall of thy body between thy soul and eternal flames. How soon may God stop thy breath! There is nothing but that between thee and hell; if that were gone, then farewell all. Thou art condemned, and the muffler is before thine eyes. God knows how soon the ladder may be turned; thou hang- est but by one rotten twined thread of thy life, over the flames of hell every hour.[15]

The similitudes multiply, each a display of inventiveness, yet each addition marks Shepard's disinclination to pursue and to develop any one image and thereby to wring from it its dramatic potential. He shifts from the image of sinners ready to fall, to a paper wall sep- arating the sinner from the flames of hell, to a ladder and thread. At times the images become in themselves fascinating; continuing, Shepard notes that devils await the sinner's soul:

> Now thy day is past, and darkness begins to overspread thy soul; now flocks of devils come into thy chamber, waiting for thy soul, to fly upon it as a mastiff dog when the door is opened. And this is the reason why most men die quietly that lived wickedly, because Satan then hath them as his own prey; like pirates, who let a ship pass that is empty of goods, they shoot commonly at them that are richly loaden. (p. 36)

We can see why the seventeenth-century Puritan sermon at times constituted a form of popular entertainment; the allusion to pirates has something of the appeal of an adventure story—yet the surprise it presents inhibits the auditor from vividly imagining himself about to be dragged off by devils storming his chamber. Such inventiveness suggests more the metaphysical conceits of Donne and Andrews than the fusion of form and content Edwards sought; it would not do if one wished to impart a sensible knowledge of the horror of hell.[16]

II

From his own experience and from his study of Locke's psychology Edwards knew that it would be highly unlikely for someone to be saved possessing only an abstract knowledge of the horrors of hell. To grasp the truth that the fires of hell are infinitely terrible, one must have an actual feeling of terror, an idea requiring a movement of the will, an idea of reflection based upon an affection. At times the evangelical preacher, it follows, should strive to induce real feelings of fear, despair, and horror, if his congregation is to have a vital sense of what damnation means. Accordingly, Edwards felt no compunction over preaching the imprecatory sermon and defended its use, saying in "The Distinguishing Marks" that "if there be really a hell of such dreadful, and neverending torments . . . and that the bigger part of men in Christian countries do actually from generation to generation fall into, *for want of a sense of the terribleness of it, and their danger of it* . . . then why is it not proper for those that have the care of souls, to take great pains to make men sensible of it?"[17] In "Some Thoughts Concerning the Revival" he added further that some ministers have been unjustly blamed for "speaking terror to them that are already under great terrors, instead of comforting them." But if what is said is true, the minister is altogether justified "to say anything to those who have never believed in the Lord Jesus Christ, to represent their case any otherwise then exceeding terrible, is not to preach the Word of God to 'em. . . . The more we bring sinners into the light, while they are miserable, and the light is terrible to them, the more likely it is that by and by the light will be joyful to them." Bring sinners to a feeling of terror, an actual idea of it, and they will know better what hell is. Only if the sinner shakes from fear will he appreciate the glorious and excellent promises of the Gospel and be saved.[18]

By 1741, the year Edwards preached at Enfield his most famous sermon, "Sinners in the Hands of an Angry God," New England congregations had been hearing about fire and brimstone for over a hundred years; to say they were inured to attempts at frightening them into heaven would seem to be decidedly an exaggeration, as the frequency of revivals touched off, at least in part, by hell-fire preaching evinces. But they were not easily moved, not by the old repertoire, the standard analogies between the tortures inflicted by kings and those by an omnipotent God, between the pain felt from an ordinary burn and that from the fire of hell. At the end of his imprecatory "The Future Punishment of the Wicked Unavoidable and Intolerable," preached three months before the Enfield sermon, Edwards acknowledged the congregation's imperturbability: "I suppose some of you have heard all that I have said with ease and quietness: it appears to you as great big sounding words, but doth not reach your hearts. You have heard such things many times: you are old soldiers, and have been too much used to the roaring of heaven's cannon, to be frighted at it."[19]

A new means had to be found to convince sinners of the scorching horrors that awaited them if they did not repent and seek the mercy of Christ. Too often sinners objected that "though it be true they have often been told of hell, yet they never say any thing of it, and therefore they cannot realize it that there is any such place."[20] The remedy Edwards tried, apparently with some frequency after 1739, consisted of exercising the imagination to make the terrors of hell more vivid than the traditional sermon was capable of making them. His primary intention was not to picture hell as a material phenomenon or to sketch devils as beings with hideous physical properties; he did not wish simply to illustrate by substituting objects of sense for spirit. His was a new aesthetic, and its purpose was to provoke affections, to draw out emotions that would be felt in hell—or heaven—in a vastly greater degree. To lead the imagination of the congregation was his method. He would have them imagine what hell or an event from Biblical history was like by reference to ordinary happenings or fictions easily imagined. This in itself was not new; the novelty of Edwards' aesthetic rested in the dramatic intensity he wrought in the sketches, the vividness of the fictions he created. He sought not to surprise with a similitude, but by the vividness of the tableau to evoke a particular emotional response. He purged his style of the multitude of diverse similes that a Shepard might employ, eliminating all but analogies that together might work to produce a controlled dramatic effect.

In "The Future Punishment of the Wicked," for instance, we see him trying to elicit a feeling of despair by use of the imagination. First he notes that it is impossible to conceive of the despair felt in hell; it has not been experienced; we have no sense knowledge of it. Then he instructs the congregation to apply imagination:

But to help your conception, imagine yourself to be cast into a fiery oven, all of a glowing heat, or into the midst of a glowing brick-kiln, or of a great furnace, where your pain would be as much greater than that occasioned by accidentally touching a coal of fire, as the heat is greater. Imagine also that your body were to lie there for a quarter of an hour, full of fire, all the while full of quick sense; what horror would you feel at the entrance of such a furnace! And how long would that quarter of an hour seem to you! If it were to be measured by a glass, how long would the glass seem to be running! And after you had endured it for one minute, how overbearing would it be to you to think that you had it to endure the other fourteen![21]

He has his audience imagine by stages, first conceiving what it must be like to be thrown into a furnace, then what one must feel knowing how long the pain will last. He does not attempt to picture hell as such but is concerned with the feelings of horror and despair that occur with the realization that the terrible pain will be for eternity. Each detail in the passage aids in the imagining of the horrors to be faced.

Occasionally Edwards employs similar methods in sermons that are more instructional than hortatory. In "The Folly of Looking Back in Fleeing Out of Sodom" he adds fictional details to the Biblical account to make the episode more conceivable. Citing Genesis 19:23, "The sun was risen upon the earth when Lot entered into Zoar," he embellishes with, "It seems to have been a fair morning in Sodom before it was destroyed. It seems that there were no clouds to be seen, no appearance of any storm at all, much less of a storm of fire and brimstone."[22] An example of more extended application of the imagination occurs in a sermon about Noah, delivered in 1740, and entitled "The Manner in which the Salvation of the Soul Is to be Sought." Here Edwards recounts, with various imaginative conjectures, the story of the building of the ark. "It is not probable that any of that wicked generation would put to a finger to help forward such a work, which doubtless they believed was merely the fruit of Noah's folly, without full wages." More conjectures follow: Noah must have been very rich to undertake such an enterprise as the construction of the immense ark; he probably spent his fortune on the project. He continues:

For a man to undertake such a vast piece of work, under a notion that it should be the means of saving him when the world should be destroyed, it made him the continual laughing stock of the world. When he was about to hire workmen, doubtless all laughed at him, and we may suppose, that though the workmen consented to work for wages, yet they laughed at the folly of him who employed them. When the ark was begun, we may suppose that every one that passed by and saw such a huge hulk stand there, laughed at it, calling it "Noah's folly."[23]

Prefacing his suppositions with a *doubtless*, a *we may suppose*, or a *probably*, Edwards constructs a remarkably vivid scene from the relatively stark Biblical account. Then he applies the lesson of the story to the great problem, men not believing the Bible because of not having sense knowledge of what it teaches. In Noah's time, he points out, men had the same difficulty: "What was the reason that none of the many millions then upon earth believed what Noah said, but this, that it was a strange thing, that no such thing had ever before been known?" They could not conceive of what Noah warned. The message is dire; those who cannot or will not conceive of what the Bible warns also will face destruction; and so one's spiritual fate may well hinge upon one's power of imagination.

III

Edwards draws from the scriptural text for "Sinners in the Hands of an Angry God" the same lesson; the Israelites, like all sinners, faced imminent destruction, but they refused to realize their peril, remaining "void of counsel, having no understanding in them."[24] His theme is of the fell consequences of not conceiving adequately the meaning of God's threat to destroy those who do not obey him. To convey a sense of dread and thereby to provide an idea of the horrors of hell, Edwards employs the imagination to construct the fiction of a pit of fire over which the auditor hangs suspended.

Edwin H. Cady, in his analysis of "Sinners" as a work of art, claims that the images in the sermon taken from the Bible usually fail, that they were too familiar to the Enfield congregation to awaken them. "Inescapably," he writes, "Edwards was addicted to the use of Biblical quotation and allusion with suggestive, figurative intent. Occasionally he was successful, especially with the text of his sermon. But for the most part he fails when he depends upon them rather than upon the careful, artistic elaboration of the symbols of his own imagination."[25] Many if not most of the images do indeed derive from the Bible and were habitually called upon in evangelical preaching. Assuming, then, that Edwards' task was to move an audience calloused by the traditional sermon, the question is whether his reliance upon such imagery was indeed no more than an unfortunate addiction. An alternative explanation is that he uses the traditional images unconventionally, not, that is, to surprise the congregation in the manner encouraged by the old aesthetic. Rather, in "Sinners" Edwards combines the old Biblical images into a harmonic, or organic, whole, each in keeping with the others, so that together they elicit a sense, or *affectionate,* response. He does not, like Shepard, mix pirates with devils. The images of "Sinners" display harmony and consistency rather than startling, conspicuous ingenuity.

The Enfield sermon is not so much an exposition of doctrine as an elaboration of the significance of a trope, "their foot shall slide in due time" (Deut. 32:35). Edwards chose for his text not the segment of the verse that warns of the awful consequences of not obeying God ("the day of their calamity is at hand"), but its figurative representation. His concern in the sermon is not to expound theology by enumerating the various logical reasons and implications that support a doctrine, but to analyze the implications of the image, all the while keeping it before the auditor as a concrete representation of his spiritual condition. It implies, he states, that the destruction of the Israelites, brought about by themselves, contingent upon the will of God, would be sudden. All this, which otherwise would be mere abstraction, the sinner can grasp in the image if he exercises his imagination and so feels the sense of unexpectedness and helplessness one has in falling. Such a sensation can stand in his mind for the response he would feel if he could actually perceive his spiritual condition. The image of sliding from the edge of a slippery pit, however, does not remain the central fiction of the sermon. Edwards uses it as a foundation for constructing the image partially signified in the title of the sermon, that of the sinner's being held in the hands of an angry God over the pit of hell.

He establishes this image when elaborating upon the principle that "nothing . . . keeps wicked men at any one moment out of hell but the mere pleasure of God."[26] He links each part of the image to a principal point of the doctrine. To signify the power and "arbitrary mercy" of God, he employs the synecdoche of the hands of God; the opposi-

tion of God to sin he represents anthropomorphically as anger; the
nature of sin in man he identifies with "brimstone":

> There are in the souls of wicked men those hellish *principles* [Edwards'
> italics] reigning, that would presently kindle and flame out into hell fire,
> if it were not for God's restraints. There is laid in the very nature of
> carnal men, a foundation for the torments of hell. There are those cor-
> rupt principles, in reigning power in them, and in full possession of
> them, that are seeds of hell fire . . . and if it were not for the restraining
> hand of God upon them, they would soon break out, they would flame
> out. . . . (p. 158)

That the sinner faces innumerable threats to his life, that he exists
amidst innumerable possibilities of dying, Edwards signifies with the
image of the sinner walking "over the pit of hell on a rotten cover-
ing" (p. 159). Thus Edwards uses his imagery symbolically to depict
the spiritual condition of the sinner, his being totally dependent upon
God's arbitrary mercy, his own sins bringing about his destruction.
He concludes the doctrinal portion of the sermon by bringing together the images associated with the principles he has presented as if
they were a conclusion to a discourse; yet they compose a picture, a
fiction of the imagination that reveals the sinner's condition: "So
that, thus it is that natural men are held in the hand of God, over the
pit of hell; they have deserved the fiery pit, and are already sentenced
to it; and God is dreadfully provoked. . . . The devil is waiting for
them, hell is gaping for them, the flames gather and flash about
them . . . (p. 161).

While it is true that Edwards does introduce other images that do
not directly pertain to the pit, the fire, and the hands of God, he is
careful to subordinate them to the dominant motif. In the beginning
of the sermon, for example, he presents a cluster of diverse Biblical
images to suggest the vast disproportion between the power of God
and that of men:

> The strongest have no power to resist him, nor can any deliver out of his
> hands. —He is not only able to cast wicked men into hell, but he can
> most easily do it. Sometimes an earthly prince meets with a great deal of
> difficulty to subdue a rebel, who has found means to fortify himself,
> and has made himself strong by the numbers of his followers. But it is
> not so with God. There is no fortress that is any defense from the power
> of God. Though hand join in hand, and vast multitudes of God's en-
> emies combine and associate themselves, they are easily broken in

pieces. They are as great heaps of light chaff before the whirlwind; or
large quantities of dry stubble before devouring flames. We find it easy
to tread on and crush a worm that we see crawling on the earth; so it is
easy for us to cut or singe a slender thread that any thing hangs by: thus
easy is it for God, when he pleases, to cast his enemies down to hell.
(p. 156)

Each image is appropriate to suggest great power easily overwhelming something less; none stands out as a surprise. The dominant
image of the fiery pit recedes into the background but never entirely
fades: "devouring flames" recalls it; "to cut or singe a slender
thread" foreshadows the image in the Application of the sinner
hanging by so feeble a support; the figure of God casting sinners into
the pit returns to re-establish the controlling figure. Usually, however, the images in the sermon fit together tightly. Thus in the Application Edwards extends a metaphor of the forces of nature. "The
earth would not bear you one moment," we are told; the sun and air
do not willingly serve the sinner. God's wrath hangs above the rep-
robates' heads in the form of "black clouds" "big with thunder," but
he holds back "his rough wind." Continuing with images from nature, Edwards paints the wrath of God as "great waters that are
dammed for the present." Again the series of images resolves in a return to the primary motif; God's "hand" holds the waters back as it
holds the sinner over the pit, temporarily saving him from the fires he
deserves (pp. 162–63). An equally important display of Edwards'
ordering of images occurs at the beginning of the Application. Here
in the direct address to "unconverted persons in this congregation,"
we are told we will fall "if God should withdraw his hand," yet our
wickedness makes us "as it were heavy as lead" (p. 162). The use of
lead to signify the weight of the sinner's wickedness harmonizes, or
unites, with the central image; only God can bear such a weight; so
weighted down, the sinner, powerless, will fall when God lets go.

The degree to which Edwards succeeded in his sermon at Enfield
has become legendary. The inhabitants had remained unmoved
while people in neighboring towns were swept by a revival. They
were "very secure, loose and vain," and when ministers from other
places entered the meetinghouse to hear Edwards preach, "the
people hardly conducted themselves with common decency." But before he finished, "there was such a breathing of distress and weeping,
that the preacher was obliged to speak to the people and desire si-

lence, that he might be heard."[27] The reaction of Nehemiah Strong, one of Edwards' parishioners in Northampton, to the depiction of the last judgment sketched in one of the sermons intended for the *History of Redemption* underscores the effect a proper application of the imagination might achieve upon a New England congregation long used to imprecatory sermons: "his own mind was wrought up to such a pitch that he expected without one thought to the contrary the awful scene to be unfolded on that day and in that place. Accordingly, he waited with the deepest and the most solemn solicitude to hear the trumpet sound and the archangel call; to see the graves open, the dead arise, and the Judge descend in the glory of his Father, with all his holy angels; and was deeply disappointed when the day terminated and left the world in its usual state of tranquillity."[28]

In "Sinners" Edwards made imaginable the doctrine that damnation awaits those who remain unconverted; he expressed it in images so suited one to another, so carefully bound together, that his audience knew as they had never known before the tenuousness of their existence and the nature of the punishment that was in store. The fiction of being suspended over the pit of hell was so real, the feeling that at any moment they might drop so intense, that they had sensations of dread and terror, giving them real ideas. They had a sense of the consequences of not availing themselves of the mercy of Christ. In the beginning of the Application Edwards wrote:

> This that you have heard is the case of every one of you that are out of Christ.—That world of misery, that lake of burning brimstone, is extended abroad under you. There is the dreadful pit of the glowing flames of the wrath of God; there is hell's wide gaping mouth open; and you have nothing to stand upon, nor any thing to take hold of; there is nothing between you and hell but the air; it is only the power and mere pleasure of God that holds you up. (p. 162)

The passage has a directness that emphasizes the importance of —and perhaps we should add, confidence in—the degree to which the central image has been established. The audience is directly addressed with the pronoun *you* and told, not obliquely with a simile but with the explicitness of metaphor, that it hangs over a pit. Clearly we are meant to believe in the fiction so carefully wrought, to suspend, as Coleridge would have it, our disbelief.[29]

IV

Occasionally a student of Edwards detects signs pointing to his interest in romance. Perry Miller, for instance, characterizes the accounts in "A Faithful Narrative" of Abigail Hutchinson and Phebe Bartlet as being "little romances in the key of Richardson."[30] Examining the "Personal Narrative," John Griffith finds a "successful piece of poetic fiction" having "the flat, stylized quality of a romance."[31] And Thomas H. Johnson remarks that Edwards "was a man widely enough read to know that literature could sometimes be a part of one's 'improvement,' and that novels or 'romances' might well form a part of literature," and cites Dwight's claim that he read *Sir Charles Grandison* with notable pleasure.[32] Indeed Dwight says:

> About the time of his leaving Northampton, he received one of the works of Richardson, (Note: *Sir Charles Grandison*. I had this anecdote through his eldest son [Timothy Edwards]) which he read with deep interest, and regarded as wholly favourable to good morals and purity of character. The perusal of it led him to attempt the formation of a more correct style, his previous inattention to which, he then deeply regretted.[33]

Unfortunately, perhaps, Dwight's story does not hold up well: Edwards left Northampton in 1751 and was rusticated in Stockbridge for at least two years before *The History of Sir Charles Grandison* began to appear in 1753.[34] Nevertheless considerable evidence exists to demonstrate Edwards' abiding attention to romance, at least in the later years of his life. In his "Catalogue," a notebook listing books he wished to read, he mentions several novels and occasionally has jotted down a short, summary comment from the review providing the information.

The remarks about romances Edwards copied into the "Catalogue" indicate his interest in using art to serve piety. He records, for example: "Clarissa [1747–48] a Romance in several volumes highly commended in the Scots Magazine of Novem. 1749 as tending much to promote virtue and piety said in the New York Gazette May 28, 1753 to be written by one Harlow & to be in 8 volumes."[35] Henry Fielding's *Amelia* (1751) has the distinction of being "commended in *Monthly Review* for Decem. 1751 as recommending Virtue and Conjugal Love" (MS, p. 28). He has two entries on *Pam-*

ela, or Virtue Rewarded (1740); one is lined through, which may or may not reveal that he managed to obtain and read it;[36] he notes the reviewer's speaking of it "as an *interesting original* worthy to be spoken of in terms of high respect which has afforded entertainment to Readers of all Ranks" (MS, pp. 26, 31). In another entry he records: "The aventures of Telemachus [1699] written by the Late arch-Bishop of Cambray which Chambers says is a work never enough to be applauded under the word *Romance*" (MS, p. 12). This item in the "Catalogue" is of special interest, for it shows that Edwards read the article on romance in Ephraim Chambers' *Cyclopaedia*, which cites the novel by François De Salignac de la Mothe-Fénelon as an example. Reading Chambers' article Edwards found a definition of romance and a statement of its moral purpose:

> M. Fontenelle calls *romances*, poems in prose; and Boffu is not averse to their being admitted as poetical pieces. . . . The just notion . . . of a romance, is, that it is a discourse invented with art to please and improve the mind, and to form or mend the manners, by instructions disguised under the allegory of an action or series of actions, related in prose, in a delightful, probable, yet surprizing manner. . . .
>
> A just *romance* consists of two parts, *viz.* a moral, as its foundation and end; and a fable, or action, as the superstructure and means.[37]

Edwards' attention late in his life to the early novel evinces his continuing interest in the potential of art to further religion. Conceivably his closely attending reviews of fiction bespeaks the lines of thought developed before his twentieth birthday in the notes on "The Mind." He had discovered previously, before learning in the late 1740s or early 1750s of Richardson and Fielding, that art could serve piety. He knew it could evoke a sensation resembling the religious experience, capable of providing a sensible idea to substitute in its place. As a vehicle of the imagination, art could represent to the mind situations never actually experienced and produce feelings important to religion, such as terror at the prospect of the fires of hell.

The romances he read about in reviews must have provoked a sense of recognition; they bore some resemblance to what he himself had written, sometime after 1735, in the idealized sketches of Abigail Hutchinson and Phebe Bartlet. Edwards perhaps hoped such books, very difficult to obtain in Northampton and Stockbridge, could further his knowledge of the employment of art to instill a feeling of delight similar, in a small but vital degree, to the sense of sweetness, or *suavitas*, in the discovery of divine beauty. They were instances of the imagination's being used to give form to virtue, permitting the abstract and immaterial to be conceived. But whereas Pamela and Clarissa were idealized heroines of British middle-class morality, Abigail and Phebe were embodiments of the ideal of New England piety, as Edwards understood it; their virtue consisted not of fending off the illicit attention of roués but in their "ravishing view of the glory of God appearing in the trees, and growth of the fields, and other works of God's hands."[38] Edwards most successfully deploys elements of romance earlier, however, in the idealized portrait usually taken to be of the young girl of thirteen who was to become his wife, Sarah Pierrepont.[39]

In the manner of a romance, the prose-poem, written in 1723, distances the reader from its heroine to establish her as embodying the ideal of virtue. Edwards omits such details—for instance, her size or the color of her hair—as tend to individualize and to make her seem less than a wondrously spiritual being. Even her name is omitted, for its disclosure might make her seem enclosed by human conventions and bound by ties of family. She exists as an ideal rather than as ordinary mortal, a status suggested in the formulaic beginning of the piece: "They say there is a young lady in [New Haven]. . . ." The *they say* like the *once upon a time* of a fairy tale, suggests a special renown; her excellence has become famous, for she surpasses ordinary mortals. The suggestion of her location serves further to emphasize her uniqueness—only in this one place, presumably New Haven, will the remarkable, rare creature be found. She is so touched by the divine that in comparison we ordinary people may try basely to tempt her: "And you could not persuade her to do anything wrong or sinful, if you would give her all the world, lest she should offend this great being."

The central romantic motif in the piece lies in the depiction of the relation between the young lady and God as the love affair between a great and mysterious lord, or sovereign, and his brave, totally devoted mistress. He visits her only at *certain seasons*, times that ordinary men cannot predict. He is described simply as "that great Being who made and rules the world," as if he were a most exalted noble governing a vast domain. The distinction of the young lady owes to

the noble personage's favoring of her, to her being *beloved b*
Shortly she will be taken to his kingdom, and their love will be
summated. As Norman Grabo points out, there are sexual implic
tions in the line telling of their eventual union: "there she is to dwell
with him, and to be ravished with his love and delight forever."[40]

The portrait depicts its subject as something of a mystery, her
transcendence of ordinary human nature making her somewhat un-
fathomable. We are never told precisely what her experiences of
"this great God" are, but are left to wonder what is the "strange
sweetness in her mind." We do not learn when or why the Being will
come to her, or what it means that "in some way or other invisible"
he communicates with her. The rites of their union are unknown to
us, so that excluded we stand in awe of her and the strange events
that surround her.

In portraying the lady romantically as remote from ordinary
people, Edwards not only establishes her as an ideal but underscores
at the same time the Calvinistic quality of her piety. She stands apart
because she renounces the things of this world and chooses instead a
meditative, intimate relation of an Augustinian sort with God. Unlike Pamela, whose chastity unexpectedly earns her a good marriage,
Edwards' heroine gives up the world, preferring solitude in order to
taste the sense of the heart. As will so many American heroes to follow in the next two centuries, who explore the wilderness and abhor
society (albeit with increasingly secular motives), she "loves to be
alone, walking in the fields and groves." She firmly believes in the
renunciation of all in this world for the next. Lest we think Edwards'
young lady quite impossible even in his own day, it is well to recall
that David Brainerd, on his deathbed dying of tuberculosis, said to
his sweetheart, one of Edwards' daughters, "Dear Jerusha, are you
willing to part with me?—I am quite willing to part with you. . . . But
we shall spend a happy eternity together."[41]

The portrait of the young lady possibly was one of Edwards' own
lively pictures, an imagining that helped him conceive of spiritual
beauty. Perry Miller writes that Edwards' story lies between it and
"Sinners in the Hands of an Angry God."[42] Indeed they display the
span, in a sense, of his theology and his imagination, from the hell
that taxes our tolerance and so preoccupies his detractors, to the
aesthetic that delights us with its charm and originality. Each piece

conviction that religion is essentially a matter of
...s, for each attempts to elicit an emotional re-
...rnish an idea of spiritual matters.

Edwards' compositions have artistic dimen-
...was a conscious artist would be an exaggera-
...will bear close, critical analysis—though more
...ve received such attention, among them *The*
, *...rue Virtue*. It would also be an overstatement to claim
that art culminates Edwards' aesthetics; yet he addresses, though not
at length, the subject of art and its import. It was in his eyes one
source of the beauty that as a type parallels spiritual harmony and
thereby serves as an aide to human comprehension. His own artistic
efforts were not extensive; many of them may have been minor ex-
periments to test his aesthetic theories, or were reflections of his scientific, theological curiosity—not ends in themselves. The ambition
that marks his youthful study of spiders, to find the laws of nature
that control material phenomena and to analyze the natural laws as
types, to an extent characterizes his brief discussions of art, and perhaps even some of his most artistic productions. But while the thrust
of Edwards' aesthetics lies not in the direction of art itself, nevertheless within the context of the Puritan tradition in America, the import he assigned to its products may well have had a profound
significance.

Chapter 5
Concluding Remarks on Edwards and the Puritan Tradition

Edwards' contribution to American literature may lie less in the artistic quality of his writings, though they occasionally exhibit estimable craftsmanship, than in the implications of his aesthetics. A few sermons, foremostly "A Divine and Supernatural Light," "Sinners in the Hands of an Angry God," and some lyrical passages, as the prose poem about Sarah Pierrepont, and the polished treatise on *The Nature of True Virtue,* occupy an honorable place in early American literature. But the majority of Edwards' compositions more likely interest students of the history of religion and of philosophy than of belles-lettres. To a degree his aesthetics may have created a particular need within New England culture for art, but the extent of Edwards' influence, of whatever sort, remains uncertain. There are, however, indications that it differs from what previously was supposed. Alan Heimert recently has attempted to show that "in truth, the partisans of evangelical and emotional religion [of the eighteenth century] were all in some degree under the intellectual dominion of Jonathan Edwards. . . . Just as close to Edwards [as Samuel Hopkins] in idea and spirit (and perhaps closer) were the multitude of New Light and New Side preachers, Separatists and Baptists, who, despite their minor differences with Edwards, acknowledged him to be 'the greatest pillar in this part of ZION'S BUILDING.' " Edwards' aesthetics, Heimert maintains, contained a *radical import,* a *social vision* that led to a demand for a reorganization of society.[1] Heimert's thesis remains an intriguing possibility but has not as yet received wide acceptance by historians. He presents a large quantity of evidence but analyzes little of it in sufficient detail. Roland A. Delattre recently

emonstrate that indeed there are "political im-
ances" emanating from Edwards' aesthetics.[2]
degree of influence the artistic implications of
have exerted remains to be explored. In short,
or students of early American literature is
ort of art, beauty, imagination, and nature in
significantly affected the Puritan tradition. If Edwards
was known by more than just *The Freedom of the Will,* if the aesthetic character of his thought endured in Calvinist circles, then the possibility exists that his emphasis on natural beauty as a type of spiritual beauty, on the essence of regeneration as the sense of the heart or as the perception of divine beauty, entered the New England tradition and even, through currently undefined channels, eventually came to help shape the thinking of Ralph Waldo Emerson.[3]

To date research into Edwards' followers, known by various names—New Lights, the Edwards School—generally indicates an indifference to his aesthetics *per se.* Delattre claims that "even his closest followers never fully shared or appropriated unto themselves his conviction that in the experience of beauty we are given the most critical disclosure of the nature of reality" (p. 22). Yet Heimert's study suggests a widespread, at least rudimentary, understanding of some of the central points of his system.[4]

Edwards' principal followers—Hopkins, Bellamy, Jonathan Edwards, Jr., Emmons, Taylor, and Tyler among others—have been almost universally decried as remarkably, if not astonishingly, dull; often they are accused of driving their congregations from the churches with the very vapidity of their pulpit discourses. Sidney Earl Mead suggests that "the history of the Edwardean, or New England, theology, as it came to be known, might well be written in terms of the extraction by these unimaginative men [the New Lights] of hard and solid metaphysical entities from Edwards' writings, which had never lacked an element of poetry, and in pushing his implications without poetic insight to their logical, though bitter, limits."[5] Robert L. Ferm agrees, claiming that "the Neo-Platonic and mystic frame of Mind" that characterized Edwards' thought is utterly lacking in the work of his unoriginal disciples, who cast his aesthetic principles into *legal images.*[6] Writing a little over a hundred years after Edwards' death, Calvin Ellis Stowe, who declared himself "in the main a Calvinist of the Jonathan Edwards School," suggested that Edwards' theology exerted a fatal fascination, charming his followers into a slavish dependence upon his writings and into inept attempts to construct metaphysical systems. In the days of Lyman Beecher, writes Stowe, "President Edwards, and not the Apostle Paul, was the leading theologian." There was a degeneracy; no longer was there careful reading of the Bible in the original tongues; human invention and not "the inspired utterances of God" became the norm, and "the prime cause of this degeneracy lay in the fascination and success of Edwards' metaphysical writings."[7]

Of Edwards' disciples, Samuel Hopkins (1721–1803) is thought to have most faithfully transmitted the master's teachings, which is not to deny that he made significant departures. In discussing connections between Edwards and Emerson, students of the Puritan tradition note that Hopkins was the student of Edwards and the teacher of William Ellery Channing (1780–1842), who in turn was the spiritual mentor of Emerson. Notoriously Hopkins illustrated Edwards' teachings on true virtue with the assertion that the saint felt a willingness to be damned for the glory of God, such was his selflessness, the feeling of harmonious inclination of his will towards God. In *The Minister's Wooing,* in which Hopkins is the foundation for the principal character, Harriet Beecher Stowe represents the awesome psychological burden and the spiritual inspiration of his ideal; in the novel Mary Scudder learns from his teaching "how blest it is to lose herself in that eternal Love and Beauty of which all earthly fairness and grandeur are but the dim type, the distant shadow...," thereby recalling the import Edwards assigned to the experience of beauty, as that of art or of nature, as an earnest of the aesthetic sensation to be experienced in heaven.[8]

William Ellery Channing regarded Hopkins ambivalently. "His delivery in the pulpit," Channing once wrote, "was the worst I ever met with. Such tones never came from any human voice within my hearing. He was the very ideal of bad delivery." And though finding Hopkins' theology in the main to be equally unsavory—"stern and appalling" he calls it—Channing nevertheless testifies to the powerful influence of the doctrine of benevolence: "I need not be ashamed to confess the deep impression which this system made on my youthful mind. I am grateful to this stern teacher for turning my thoughts and heart to the claims and majesty of impartial, universal benevolence.[9] One essential ingredient of Edwards' aesthetics thus was available at the inception of transcendentalism, as interpreted, presented, and practiced by Hopkins (both Channing and Stowe found admirable the extent to which he lived by what he preached).[10]

There have been diverse attempts, several of them distinguished, to define the Puritan, or New England, tradition in American literature, or to reveal points of connection between the two principals, Edwards and Emerson. Avoiding what he considered to be the adulation of the ancestor worshipers and the diatribes of the Puritan baiters (such as H. L. Mencken), Kenneth Murdock pioneered with a lecture delivered in 1927 by identifying some primary characteristics. Though mainly concerned with establishing the common factors among Puritan writers, he desired at the same time to define, insofar as possible, the tradition they inspired. He singled out Emerson as nearer to the original Puritans than any other writer of his time in that "he revolted against dead form and system; his test for everything was rooted in the moral, and he preached always the morality which proceeds from the sincere belief of the individual transcending law merely as law."[11] The Puritan tradition divides into two components, Murdock explained: "the heritage of later Puritanism, which wields rules into systems, and the other, nearer to the nonconformist spirit of the first settlers on Massachusetts shores, which also makes moral values and Biblical precept supreme, but conceives of them not merely as grim idols cut in the stone of inherited reverence but as part of the expression of the enthusiasm and richness of the spirit of man. This view dethroned kings and settled wilderness, and must be implicit in a Puritan tradition worthy of the name" (p. 101).

In his well-known essay "From Edwards to Emerson," Perry Miller in 1940 expanded upon the conception of the great division, finding on one side "a piety, a religious passion, the sense of an inward communication and of the divine symbolism of nature" and on the other "an ideal of social conformity, of law and order, of regulation and control."[12] The side of piety in the *dual heritage* contained the potentiality for the pantheism and mysticism of the Transcendentalists, and Jonathan Edwards, despite his intentions, in the texture if not logic of his theology, opened Pandora's box: "If God is diffused through nature, and the substance of man is the substance of God, then it may follow that man is divine, that nature is the garment of the Over-Soul, that man must be self-reliant, and that when he goes into the woods the currents of Being will indeed circulate through him" (pp. 195–96). Once Calvinist theology faded from the scene, according to Miller, then the pantheism and mysticism of Transcendentalism could take shape. When it was collected into *Errand into the Wilderness,* Miller prefaced his essay with the declaration that he was not arguing for an "organic evolution of ideas from Edwards to Emerson" but that he hoped to outline "certain basic continuities." His approach, or interest, was by and large that of the intellectual historian, who examines the formal statements of ideas and places them within a broad context. He looked for continuities that bore upon major philosophic issues, such as Transcendentalism itself. On the other hand, Murdock in his quest for themes and attitudes in American literature tended to be more empirical; he attended more the informal tenets of faith than explicit canon, looking for ambiance rather than the evolution of intellectual positions.

The definition of the Puritan tradition and of the connection between Edwards and Emerson has seen further refinement in recent years. Ursula Brumm, for instance, in *American Thought and Religious Typology,* has pointed to other denominators, such as the belief in the unique spiritual role for America, and to the common assumptions about nature that stem from "the continuous development of modes of thought of a single cultural tradition."[13] Of late, William A. Clebsch notes that "Edwards and Emerson and James (and other religious thinkers) resisted the moralistic spirituality toward which America's chief religious heritage, Puritanism, almost inevitably tends"; instead they affirmed an aesthetic spirituality.[14] For the most part Clebsch's discussion proceeds on too general a level to be compelling, but while it does not define the aesthetic legacy, it is valuable in the recognition that Edwards "thrust the Puritan tradition forward" into the belief that "one's life [should] become an act of beauty."[15]

The Puritan tradition as a whole, and specifically the nexus between Edwards and Emerson, still remains largely undefined. Conceivably, certain resemblances between the Calvinist and the Transcendentalist are coincidental, independent of a shared cultural background, perhaps mostly an accidental matter of personality. Both Edwards and Emerson, for instance, display a penchant for aesthetics, a curiosity as to what constitutes harmony and a wonder as to the extent it characterizes the values of both God and man. Emerson recalls passages from the "Mind" when he ponders: "It is the perpetual effort of the mind to seek relations between the multitude of facts under its eye, by means of which it can reduce them to some order."[16] Edwards didn't for a moment dream of taking a step closer to the edge of relativism, of saying that even scientific theories and sacred theologies themselves proceed from the instinct to harmonize, yet he too emphasized that the mind orders objects by the principles of harmony. For whatever reason, from the time of Edwards a preoccupation with aesthetics characterizes the pietistic side of the Puritan tradition. Later, George Santayana would plunge over the edge by breaking through the barriers Emerson had erected against relativism and solipsism; no longer would a multifaceted absolute inscribe the truths man perceives with his artistic eye, serving as a parameter that harmonizes the truths the seer perceives; instead, a system of thought, as a religious creed, is seen as only the internally harmonious expression of man's aesthetic instinct, not as a description of *reality*.

Some apparent connections between the thought of Edwards and that of Emerson undoubtedly owe to the careful study each made of Locke's sensationalism. The *Essay* sculptured the thinking of both into resemblant shapes at certain points. Emerson, as had Edwards before him, regarded nature from a dual perspective, sensationalism and Puritanism, and concluded that it is ordained to furnish the mind with ideas. And he too expressed the function of nature in terms of Puritan typology, to serve emblematically as "the terminus or the circumference of the invisible world."[17]

Certain other links between Edwards and Emerson seem to derive from Puritan principles to which each was exposed. The themes of perception and experience, for instance, stand out among the traditional Puritan conceptions that appear in the writings of both. To an extent, regeneration—according to Calvinism—verily consists of the power, entrusted through grace, to perceive the quality of mercy that lies in the Biblical promises of salvation. The ability to perceive depends upon the faculty of the will, upon the responses within its capacity. Everyone must see for him- or herself the truth embodied in Scripture in order to be saved, and the poignant realization of the Gospel promise constitutes the saint's firsthand experience, his experimental knowledge of God's wonderful mercy. Edwards redefined the doctrine somewhat, adding a dimension that endured in its appeal to the time of Emerson and beyond: the saint perceives, and so experiences, through the sense of the heart the beauty of holiness, or spirituality—ultimately the consent (harmony) of regenerate will to Being. To be sure, Emerson's system held the spiritual truths or laws perceived through regenerate vision to be more complex than what seventeenth-century Puritanism or even Edwards allowed. But the outlines of his teaching conform to Puritan tradition: "perception differs from Instinct by adding the Will. Simple percipiency is the virtue of space, not of man."[18] Emerson emphasizes the uniqueness of the individual's point of view, or *angle of vision,* asking, in the "Natural History of Intellect," "What is life but the angle of vision?" (p. 10). In the essay "Society" he underscores the distinctly individual nature of perception with, "But beside this generic nature every man has an individual nature. He is differenced both in person and in nature from every other man that ever existed, by having the common faculties under a bias, or determination of character altogether new and original. In him, under him, is the same world as another beholds; but it is the world seen from a new point of view; the more deeply he drinks of the common soul, the more decided does his individuality become. He sees what no other ever saw."[19] Emerson planted in the Puritan tradition a conception of perception that would flower in the novels of Henry James, who narrated his tales within the framework of a character's ability to see, who delineated meticulously the extent of his spiritual perception of moral beauty. As had his Puritan forefathers, Emerson preached that every man must perceive spiritual truth for himself, that without such direct, felt knowledge there is no real belief:

> when we have broken our god of tradition, and ceased from our god of rhetoric, then may God fire the heart with his presence. It is the doubling of the heart itself, nay, the infinite enlargement of the heart with a power of growth to a new infinity on every side. It inspires in man an infallible trust. He has not the conviction, but the sight, that the best is the true, and may in that thought easily dismiss all particular uncertainties and fears, and adjourn to the sure revelation of time, the solution of his private riddles. He is sure that his welfare is dear to the heart of being.[20]

What he propounds here remarkably resembles the old Puritan doctrine of assurance, that in the wondrous response of one's own heart, or will, lies the undoubted sign that spiritual truth is perceived and that it applies to oneself. To explore here Emerson's adaptation of the romantic psychology of reason and understanding would take us afield, but it should be noted that while the Puritan notion of the sense of the heart had become to a degree obsolete, important vestiges remain in his Transcendentalism. And they suggest a closer connection to Edwards than that deriving from their shared Puritan legacy, for Emerson declares that the essence of holiness, the sign of divinity, lies in an aesthetic feeling:

> The Heart in a cultivated nature is the emotion of delight which is awakened by any manifestation of goodness. The heart in a cultivated nature is the unerring measure of genuine goodness and is not betrayed by penchants or passions to honor the semblance of goodness. . . . The heart alike in a conscious or unconscious mind is the reverence for moral beauty. That is its God. Meekly as a maiden, when that appears, it bows itself and worships.[21]

For Emerson, as for Edwards, the primary sign of divinity is beauty, and the principal motivation towards moral conduct is the apprehension of that beauty and the desire to consent to it—that is to harmonize or conform one's own will to it. For Edwards the glimpse of divine beauty leads to a disinterested benevolence, an unselfish devotion, in behavior and in intention, to God's will—which his disciples, not as incorrectly as his well-intentioned but misguided sympathizers suggest, interpreted as the willingness to be damned for the glory of God. After the time of Edwards the principle of benevolence became an important tenet of the New England tradition, and not surprisingly appears occasionally in the works of Emerson; "the emotions of benevolence and complacency which are felt towards others. . . , from the highest degree of passionate love to the lowest degree of good will they make the sweetness of life."[22] But of more importance, perhaps, in recognizing affinities between Edwards and Emerson is the espousal by the latter of an aesthetically structured universe, harmonized by the will of an artistically inspired God, to whom man regenerate consents through benevolence. Emerson also harkened back to the neoplatonic element in Augustinian piety and, as Edwards and numerous Puritans before, perceived a realm of primary being, consisting of divine goodness. Echoes of his Puritan heritage resound in a passage such as:

> Evil is merely privative not absolute. It is like cold which is the privation of heat. All evil is so much nonentity, so much death. Benevolence is ab-

solute and real. So much benevolence as a man hath so much life hath he. For all things proceed out of this same spirit which is differently named love, justice, temperance in its different applications, just as the ocean receives different names on the several shores which it washes. All things proceed out of the same spirit and all things conspire with it.[23]

For all his supposed coldness, Emerson, as did Edwards before him, embraced passionately the conception of primary being, and as Edwards, found its primary quality to be beauty; and he too believed that all other beauty is but "the herald of inward and eternal beauty."[24] He exclaimed, "I am thrilled with delight by the choral harmony of the whole. Design! It is all design. It is all beauty. It is all astonishment."[25] Virtue harmonizes the soul to the realm of primary being, Emerson taught; acts of virtue possess an aesthetic dimension, one not materially different from what Edwards described in *The Nature of True Virtue;* "a true thought," he wrote, "a worthy deed, puts him [a man] at once in harmony with the real and eternal."[26] Ironic it may seem, but Emerson, whose individualism some find offensive, made virtue out as requiring an effacement of self not dissimilar to what Edwards preached. Nature teaches the lesson: what does not conform to her laws "will be ground to powder by her omnipresent activity," the lesson being that there must be "subordination of man."[27] Emerson was Puritan enough never to doubt that "by self-renouncement a heaven of which he [a man] had no conception, begins at once in his heart;—by the high act of yielding his will, that little individual heart becomes dilated as with the presence and inhabitation of the Spirit of God."[28] For Emerson the power of the individual rests entirely upon his conforming to the divine will, becoming an expression of it; only in knowing it, its laws, does one reach salvation, and hold the power that shapes the universe.

The ideal of selflessness and benevolence that Emerson describes here in one respect certainly was not original to Edwards; self-abnegation had long existed as a prominent facet of Calvinist culture, though as a principle it perhaps did not receive the articulation that a formal doctrine would merit.[29] But Edwards interpreted the concept aesthetically, and something of his formulation (with, or in spite of, the help of the New Light theologians) passed into the Puritan tradition, occasionally to surface not only in the writings of Channing and Emerson, but in popular novels. In *The Minister's*

Wooing, Harriet Beecher Stowe, not only a participant in but an historian of the tradition (as were Hawthorne and James), attempts to picture the vitality of Edwards' ideal:

> No real artist or philosopher ever lived who has not at some hours risen to the height of utter self-abnegation for the glory of the invisible. . . . Even persons of mere artistic sensibility are at times raised by music, painting, or poetry to a momentary trance of self-oblivion, in which they would offer their whole being before the shrine of an invisible loveliness. These hard old New England divines were the poets of metaphysical philosophy, who built systems in an artistic fervor, and felt self exhale from beneath them as they rose into the higher regions of thought.
>
> It was easy enough for Mary to believe in self-renunciation, for she was one with a born vocation for martyrdom; and so, when the idea was put to her of suffering eternal pains for the glory of God and the good of being in general, she responded to it with a sort of sublime thrill. . . .[30]

As the tone of the passage suggests, Stowe appreciated the richness of the Edwardsian aesthetic legacy, though she knew well, also, the severe mental anguish its conceptions could elicit. She perceived a moral beauty in renunciation for the sake of benevolence, as did James, who portrayed some noble as well as some pathetic "renunciations" of New England heroines.

The role Edwards assigned to art as a means to conceptualize spiritual sensations appears also to have become absorbed into the Puritan tradition. Art he realized could function as an *earnest,* or foreshadowing, of the sensation of spiritual beauty to be felt in heaven. Several times in the course of *The Minister's Wooing,* Stowe outlines a similar function. At one point she alludes to Plato as "an old heathen" who approximated something of Christian truth when observing that "the soul, by the power of music or poetry, or the sight of beauty hath her remembrance quickened. . . ," but she underscores that the Christian conception differs: "Let us look up in fear and reverence and say, 'God is the great maker of romance. . . . He is the great Poet of life.' Every impulse of beauty, of heroism . . . is God's breath, God's impulse, God's reminder to the soul that there is something higher, sweeter, purer, yet to be attained." Such impulses are but "foreshadowings of heaven."[31] Stowe reveals the impact Edwards' theology had upon her when she attempts to explain the religious function of art: "There is a ladder to heaven, whose base God has placed in human affections, tender instincts, symbolic feelings, sacraments of love, through which the soul rises higher and higher, refining as she goes, till she outgrows the human, and changes, as she rises, into the image of the divine." Such earthly delight is but "the dim type, the distant shadow" (p. 87). Though couched in Platonic phrasing, the substance of her comments points to Edwards; affections felt toward beauty and love of a natural order provide a glimpse of the emotions to be experienced in heaven. As Emerson noted, "the contemplation of a work of great art draws us into a state of mind which may be called religious. It conspires with all exalted sentiments."[32]

In their concluding remarks, Edwards' biographers and commentators almost unfailingly express high admiration for his intelligence and sincerity and marvel at his adaptation of the New Science to his own theological ends. They praise the logical precision of his tracts and, occasionally, the economy and polish of his prose. Yet, as if by ritual, discussions of Edwards usually close on a note of ambivalence; there is disappointment that he didn't break the shackles of Calvinism and escape the provincialism of the Connecticut River Valley and lead early America, intellectually, to full participation in the enlightenment. Between the lines lurks the assumption that his diet of New England Calvinism stunted his growth artistically and philosophically. Perhaps we should question the extent to which our estimation of Edwards should depend upon criteria external to his own values and purposes; but allowing the standard yardstick of achievement—influence and power—to measure his accomplishment, we may wonder if Edwards' stature isn't taller than previously suspected. He formulated an aesthetic that, certainly by implication, made large provision for art, that explicitly provided for the importance of the beauty of nature. Ideas about moral beauty, about the importance of perception, and about the signs of spiritual truth, appear in later American literature so similar to his own, that we can reasonably suppose that Edwards may have fathered them—though their precise genealogy remains a mystery.

Notes

Preface

1 In his excellent bibliographic essay, Everett H. Emerson notes the difficulties posed for literary students seeking a comprehensive knowledge of Edwards—the absence of an established text of his writings and the specialized knowledge of philosophy and theology that an understanding of his thought requires: "Jonathan Edwards," in *Fifteen American Authors Before 1900: Bibliographic Essays on Research and Criticism,* eds. R. A. Rees and E. N. Harbert (Madison, 1971), pp. 169–84. The most extensive analysis of Edwards' aesthetics is Roland A. Delattre's *Beauty and Sensibility in the Thought of Jonathan Edwards: An Essay in Aesthetics and Theological Ethics* (New Haven, 1968), which has not appreciably benefited the present discussion. Emerson appraises the work with: "It is a pity that a study likely to be of great interest to students of American literature should be so dense" (p. 179). William J. Scheick's *The Writings of Jonathan Edwards: Theme, Motif, and Style* (College Station, Texas, 1975), attempts the difficult task of a critical analysis of Edwards' writings. See also: Paul R. Baumgartner, "Jonathan Edwards: The Theory Behind His Use of Figurative Language," *Publications of the Modern Language Association of America* 78:321–25; Willis J. Buckingham, "Stylistic Artistry in the Sermons of Jonathan Edwards," *Papers on Language and Literature* 6:136–51; Edwin H. Cady, "The Artistry of Jonathan Edwards," *New England Quarterly* 22:61–72; Michael J. Colacurcio, "The Example of Edwards: Idealist Imagination and the Metaphysics of Sovereignty," in *Puritan Influences in American Literature,* ed. Emory Elliott (Urbana, 1979); John Griffith, "Jonathan Edwards as a Literary Artist," *Criticism, a Quarterly for Literature and the Arts* 15:156–73; Thomas H. Johnson, "Jonathan Edwards," in *Literary History of the United States,* ed. Robert E. Spiller, et al., 3rd ed. (London, 1963); Wilson H. Kimnach, "Jonathan Edwards' Sermon Mill," *Early American Literature* 10:167–78; Annette Kolodny, "Imagery in the Sermons of Jonathan Edwards," *Early American Literature* 7:172–82; Marc Frank Lee, "A Literary Approach to Selected Writings of Jonathan Edwards" (Ph.D. diss., University of Wisconsin/ Milwaukee, 1973); Daniel B. Shea, "The Art and Instruction of Jonathan Ed-

wards' Personal Narrative," *American Literature* 37:17–32; and Stephen J. Stein, "Jonathan Edwards and the Rainbow: Biblical Exegesis and Poetic Imagination," *New England Quarterly* 47:440–56.

2 See Norman S. Fiering's book review in *William and Mary Quarterly*, 3rd ser., 28:655–61.

3 Thomas Shepard, *God's Plot: The Paradoxes of Puritan Piety, Being the Autobiography and Journal of Thomas Shepard*, ed. Michael McGiffert (Amherst, 1972), pp. 220–21.

Chapter 1

1 Harold Simonson, "Introduction," *Selected Writings of Jonathan Edwards* (New York, 1970), p. 12.

2 John E. Smith, "Editor's Introduction," *Religious Affections*, by Jonathan Edwards, in The Works of Jonathan Edwards, Yale edition, vol. 2 (New Haven, 1959), p. 30.

3 Ibid., p. 32; Emily S. Watts, "Jonathan Edwards and the Cambridge Platonists" (Ph.D. diss., University of Illinois, 1963).

4 Herbert W. Schneider, *A History of American Philosophy* (New York, 1946), p. 13; Conrad Wright, *The Beginnings of Unitarianism in America* (Boston, 1955), pp. 144f.

5 Clarence H. Faust and Thomas H. Johnson, "Introduction," *Jonathan Edwards, Representative Selections*, 2nd ed. (New York, 1962), p. xxxiv; Claude A. Smith, "Jonathan Edwards and 'The Way of Ideas,' " *Harvard Theological Review* 59:153–73. Cf. Douglas J. Elwood, *The Philosophical Theology of Jonathan Edwards* (New York, 1960), pp. 121, 135; Paul Helm, "John Locke and Jonathan Edwards: A Reconsideration," *Journal of the History of Philosophy* 7:51–61; and David Lyttle, "The Sixth Sense of Jonathan Edwards," *Church Quarterly Review* 167:50–59.

6 Perry Miller, *Jonathan Edwards* (New York, 1949).

7 Conrad Cherry, *The Theology of Jonathan Edwards, A Reappraisal* (New York, 1966), pp. 2, 98–99.

8 William J. Scheick, *The Writings of Jonathan Edwards: Theme, Motif, and Style* (College Station, Texas, 1975), p. x.

9 See M. van Beek, *An Enquiry into Puritan Vocabulary* (Groningen, The Netherlands, 1969), pp. 66, 120, who credits the Puritans with introducing into English the variant forms of *sensible, sensibleness,* and *senselessness.* Cherry notes in passing that "the metaphor of tasting in spiritual knowledge was readily available to Edwards in his reading background: in the Scriptures, John Calvin, the seventeenth-century Puritans, and the Cambridge Platonists," but is concerned with the "Lockean twist" Edwards gave the knowledge of faith rather than with the extent of his use of previous Reformed works for the conception—this despite the justified insistence that Edwards was foremost a Calvinist (p. 21).

10 Miller, *Jonathan Edwards*, p. 252.

11 Perry Miller, *The New England Mind, the Seventeenth Century* (Boston, 1961), p. 281. See also Perry Miller and Thomas H. Johnson, *The Puritans,* 2nd ed. (New York, 1963), p. 39.

12 Miller, *The New England Mind,* p. 285.

13 John Preston, *The New Covenant,* 9th ed. (London, 1639), p. 473. In his *English Puritanism from John Hooper to John Milton* (Durham, N.C., 1968), Everett Emerson notes that "Preston was considered to excel among those Puritan preachers who used a rational approach" (p. 241).

14 See Perry Miller, "The Rhetoric of Sensation," in *Errand into the Wilderness* (Cambridge, 1964), pp. 179, 181.

15 *The Confession of Faith* (Inverness, Scotland, 1970), p. 4.

16 Quoted in Edmund S. Morgan, *The Puritan Dilemma: The Story of John Winthrop* (Boston, 1958), p. 38.

17 Thomas Hooker, *The Application of Redemption* (London, 1656), p. 63.

18 Thomas Shepard, *God's Plot: The Paradoxes of Puritan Piety, Being the Autobiography and Journal of Thomas Shepard,* ed. Michael McGiffert (Amherst, 1972), pp. 41–42.

19 Norman Fiering, "Will and Intellect in the New England Mind," *William and Mary Quarterly,* 3rd ser., 29:529.

20 Edward Taylor, "Meditation. Ps. 72. A Psalm for Solomon, 2nd series" in *The Poems of Edward Taylor,* ed. Donald E. Stanford (New Haven, 1960), pp. 102–03.

21 Shepard, *God's Plot,* p. 223.

22 William Fenner, *Works* (London, 1657), vol. 1, p. 34.

23 John Calvin, *Institutes of the Christian Religion,* ed. John T. McNeill, trans. Ford Lewis Battles (Philadelphia, 1960), I.xv.7. Except where noted, all subsequent references are to this edition. Latin and French passages are from John Calvin, *Corpus Reformatorum: Ioannis Calvini, Opera Quae Supersunt Omnia,* eds. G. Baum, E. Cunitz, E. Reuss (Brunswick, Germany, 1863), vols. 2, 3, and 4.

24 See L. Wencelius, *L'Esthetique de Calvin* (Paris, 1937).

25 Rom. 10:10, Geneva translation.

26 See Augustine, *Confessions,* trans. William Watts (London, 1968), xi.3.

27 Samuel G. Craig, ed., *Calvin and Augustine* (Philadelphia, 1956), pp. 89–90, 96.

28 Calvin, *Corpus Reformatorum,* vol. 49, p. 164.

29 Calvin, *Institutes,* III.xi.16. My translation.

30 Thomas Norton (London, 1599); John Allen (London, 1813); F. L. Battles (Philadelphia, 1960); Henry Beveridge (Edinburgh, 1845). *Corpus Reformatorum,* vol. 4, contains Calvin's French translation of the *Institutes.*

31 Conrad Cherry, in *The Theology of Jonathan Edwards* (pp. 143f.), points to the erroneous but popular assumption that in Calvinism none could know for sure if he were saved. The saint could indeed be quite confident of election; the problem lay in his feeling of assurance eventually fading and in the fear of damnation consequently returning.

32 See Calvin, *Institutes,* III.ii.12. For a summary of various passages from the *Institutes* on faith as knowledge, see H. Jackson Forstman, *Word and Spirit: Calvin's Doctrine of Biblical Authority* (Stanford, 1962), pp. 90–105.

33 John T. McNeill, *The History and Character of Calvinism* (New York, 1954), p. 116, states that enlightenment for Calvin was a matter of the heart.

34 See Vernon J. Bourke, *Will in Western Thought: An Historico-Critical Survey* (New York, 1964); Robert Middlekauff, "Piety and Intellect in Puritanism," *William and Mary Quarterly*, 3rd ser., 22:457–70; Karl Reuter, "William Ames, the Leading Theologian in the Awakening of Reformed Pietism" (1940) in *William Ames by Matthew Nethenus, Hugo Visscher, and Karl Reuter*, ed. and trans. Douglas Horton (Cambridge, 1965), pp. 174f.; J. Rodney Fulcher, "Puritans and the Passions: The Faculty Psychology in American Puritanism," *Journal of the History of the Behavioral Sciences* 9:123–39; and especially Fiering, "Will and Intellect."

35 "Paradise Lost," XII, 86–89, in *John Milton, Complete Poems and Major Prose,* ed. Merritt Y. Hughes (New York, 1957), p. 456.

36 Fiering, "Will and Intellect," p. 529.

37 William Ames, *The Marrow of Theology*, trans. John D. Eusden (Boston, 1968), I.iii.1–3.

38 John Wollebius, *The Abridgement of Christian Divinity*, trans. Alexander Ross (London, 1656), p. 7.

39 Robert Dingley, *The Spiritual Taste Described and a Glimpse of Christ Discovered* (London, 1649), pp. 45, 101.

40 Richard Sibbes, "Commentary on 2 Corinthians, Chap. IV, ver. 6," in *The Complete Works*, ed. Alexander Grosart (Edinburgh, 1862), vol. 4, pp. 334–35.

41 Wollebius, *The Abridgement*, p. 7.

42 Richard Baxter, "Mr. Baxter's Dying Thoughts upon Philippians i.23" and "The Unreasonableness of Infidelity," in *The Practical Works of the Rev. Richard Baxter*, ed. William Orme (London, 1830), vol. 18, p. 297; vol. 20, p. 202.

43 For a discussion of Ramus' technologia as a system of mnemonics, see Frances A. Yates' pioneer work, *The Art of Memory* (Chicago, 1966), pp. 231–42. For commentary on the Puritan doctrine of preparation, see Norman Pettit's *The Heart Prepared: Grace and Conversion in Puritan Spiritual Life* (New Haven, 1966).

44 Thomas Hooker, *The Soules Implantation* (London, 1637), p. 106.

Chapter 2

1 Jonathan Edwards, "The Mind," in *The Philosophy of Jonathan Edwards from His Private Notebooks*, ed. Harvey G. Townsend (Eugene, 1955), p. 31 (#11). See John Locke's *An Essay Concerning Human Understanding*, ed. Alexander Campbell Fraser (New York, 1959), II.xxii.11 and II.i.11–12. Cf. David Lyttle, "Jonathan Edwards on Personal Identity," *Early American Literature* 7:163–71.

2 Edwards, "The Mind," p. 68 (#72). Although Leon Howard reversed the order of the two entries on personal identity in his *"The Mind" of Jonathan Edwards: A Reconstructed Text* (Berkeley, 1963), Clyde Holbrook in his editor's introduction to *Original Sin*, in The Works of Jonathan Edwards, Yale edition, vol. 3, ed. John E. Smith (New Haven, 1957–), assumes, I think rightly, that the order of the

entries suggested by the manuscript numbers is correct. See *Original Sin*, pp. 78f. For Edwards' later thoughts on the subject of identity, see pp. 388f.

3 Sereno E. Dwight, *The Life of President Edwards*, vol. 1, The Works of President Edwards (New York, 1829), p. 105.

4 Jonathan Edwards, "Some Thoughts Concerning the Revival," in *The Great Awakening*, in The Works of Jonathan Edwards, Yale edition, vol. 4, ed. C. C. Goen, p. 298.

5 Norman Fiering, "Will and Intellect in the New England Mind," *William and Mary Quarterly*, 3rd. ser., 29:553.

6 John Locke, *An Essay Concerning Human Understanding*, ed. Alexander Campbell Fraser, 2 vols. (New York, 1959), introduction, p. ii.

7 Ibid., sec. i. Locke, perhaps contrary to popular belief, did not reject the contention that the mind contains *faculties*. It is "a word proper enough," he wrote, if meant to imply "no real beings in the soul" (II.xxi.6).

8 Edwards, "The Mind," p. 249 (#397).

9 Jonathan Edwards, *Freedom of the Will* in The Works of Jonathan Edwards, Yale edition, vol. 1, ed. Paul Ramsey, p. 133.

10 Jonathan Edwards, *Religious Affections*, in The Works of Jonathan Edwards, Yale edition, vol. 2, ed. John E. Smith, pp. 96–97.

11 Footnote to Locke, *Essay*, II.xx.4.

12 Jonathan Edwards, "Miscellanies," in Townsend, *The Philosophy of Jonathan Edwards*, p. 247 (#238).

13 Edwards, "Miscellanies," #782, published by Perry Miller in "Jonathan Edwards on the Sense of the Heart," *Harvard Theological Review* 41 (1948):136. Hereafter referred to as "The Sense of the Heart."

14 Jonathan Edwards, "A Divine and Supernatural Light," in *Jonathan Edwards: Representative Selections*, eds. Clarence H. Faust and Thomas H. Johnson, rev. ed. (New York, 1962), pp. 106–07.

15 Jonathan Edwards, "Christian Knowledge: Or, the Importance and Advantage of a Thorough Knowledge of Divine Truth," in *The Works of President Edwards*, eds. Edward Williams and Edward Parsons (London, 1817 ; reprint, New York, 1968), vol. 5, p. 379.

16 Edwards, "Christian Knowledge," p. 380.

17 Edwards, "Miscellanies," #539, MS, Beinecke Rare Book and Manuscript Library, Yale University.

18 Edwards, *Works*, ed. Williams and Parsons, vol. 8, pp. 119–20. See also *Religious Affections*, p. 272.

19 Ibid.

20 Jonathan Edwards, "A Personal Narrative," in *Jonathan Edwards: A Profile*, ed. David Levin (New York, 1969), p. 27. Cf. Margaret Schlaeger, "Jonathan Edwards's Theory of Perception" (Ph.D. diss., University of Illinois, 1964).

21 Edwards, *Religious Affections*, pp. 259–60.

22 Ibid.,pp. 273, 275.

23 Edwards, "Miscellanies," in Townsend, *The Philosophy of Jonathan Edwards*, p. 244 (#aa).

24 Ibid., p. 251 (#628).

25 See Ibid., p. 245 (#123) and p. 248 (#239). Cf. Sang Hyun Lee, "Mental Activity and the Perception of Beauty in Jonathan Edwards," *Harvard Theological Review* 69:369–96.

26 Edwards, "Miscellanies," #141, MS, Beinecke Rare Book and Manuscript Library, Yale University; Townsend, *The Philosophy of Jonathan Edwards*, p. 251 (#628); Edwards, *Religious Affections*, p. 281.

27 Edwards, "Miscellanies," in Townsend, *The Philosophy of Jonathan Edwards*, p. 244 (#aa).

28 Ibid.

29 Edwards, *Religious Affections*, p. 281.

30 Edwards, "Miscellanies," in Townsend, *The Philosophy of Jonathan Edwards*, pp. 246–47 (#201).

31 Edwards, "Miscellanies," #141, MS, Beinecke Rare Book and Manuscript Library, Yale University.

32 Edwards, "Miscellanies," #375, MS, Beinecke Rare Book and Manuscript Library, Yale University.

33 Miller, "The Sense of the Heart," pp. 144–45.

34 Jonathan Edwards, *Treatise on Grace and Other Posthumously Published Writings*, ed. Paul Helm (London, 1971), pp. 49–50.

35 Edwards, "Miscellanies," in Townsend, *The Philosophy of Jonathan Edwards*, pp. 142–43 (#1208).

36 Ibid., p. 193 (#f).

37 Ibid., p. 238 (#42).

38 Edwards, *Religious Affections*, p. 118.

39 Cf. Emily S. Watts, "Jonathan Edwards and the Cambridge Platonists" (Ph.D. diss., University of Illinois, 1963).

40 Augustine, *Concerning the City of God against the Pagans*, trans. Henry Bettenson (London, 1972), xi.22.

41 In *William Perkins, 1558–1602, English Puritanist*, ed. Thomas F. Merrill (The Hague, The Netherlands, 1966), p. 92.

42 Edwards, "The Mind," p. 24 (#1).

43 Ibid., p. 47 (#45).

44 Jonathan Edwards, *The Nature of True Virtue*, ed. William K. Frankena (Ann Arbor, 1960), p. 5.

45 See Thomas Schafer, "The Concept of Being in the Thought of Jonathan Edwards" (Ph.D. diss., Duke University, 1951).

46 Edwards, *Treatise on Grace*, p. 40.

47 Edwards, "A Divine and Supernatural Light," pp. 103–04.

48 Edwards, *Treatise on Grace*, p. 55.

49 Jonathan Edwards, "An Essay on the Trinity," in *Treatise on Grace*, pp. 109–10.

50 Ibid., p. 110.

51 Jonathan Edwards, "A Dissertation Concerning the End for Which God Created the World," in *Works*, ed. Williams and Parsons, p. 455.

52 Ibid., p. 459.

53 Edwards, "The Mind," p. 143 (#1208).

54 Ibid., p. 24 (#1).

55 Edwards, *Religious Affections*, p. 254.

Chapter 3

1 Jonathan Edwards, *Treatise on Grace and Other Posthumously Published Writings*, ed. Paul Helm (London, 1971), p. 68; "Some Thoughts Concerning the Revival," in *The Great Awakening*, in The Works of Jonathan Edwards, Yale edition, vol. 4, ed. C. C. Goen (New Haven, 1957–), p. 302.

2 Jonathan Edwards, *Religious Affections*, in The Works of Jonathan Edwards, Yale edition, vol. 2, ed. John E. Smith, pp. 236–37.

3 Solomon Stoddard, *Safety of Appearing* (Boston, 1729), p. 252.

4 "Sermon on Hosea ii.15 (September, 1737)," in *The Works of President Edwards*, eds. Edward Williams and Edward Parsons (London, 1817; reprint, New York, 1968), vol. 10, p. 181.

5 "The Life and Diary of the Rev. David Brainerd, with Notes and Reflections," in *Works*, ed. Williams and Parsons, vol. 3, p. 287.

6 Sereno E. Dwight, *The Life of President Edwards*, vol. 1, The Works of President Edwards (New York, 1829), pp. 76–77.

7 In Edwards, *The Great Awakening*, p. 180.

8 See Jonathan Edwards, "A Faithful Narrative," in *The Great Awakening*, p. 187.

9 Dwight, *The Life of President Edwards*, pp. 179, 185.

10 Jonathan Edwards, *Religious Affections*, in The Works of Jonathan Edwards, Yale edition, vol. 2, ed. John E. Smith, pp. 121–22.

11 See Perry Miller's introduction to Jonathan Edwards, *Images or Shadows of Divine Things* (New Haven, 1948); Ursula Brumm, "Jonathan Edwards and Ralph Waldo Emerson," in *American Thought and Religious Typology* (New Brunswick, 1970), pp. 86–108; and Mason I. Lowance, Jr., " 'Images or Shadows of Divine Things' in the Thought of Jonathan Edwards," in *Typology and Early American Literature*, ed. Sacvan Bercovitch (Amherst, 1972), pp. 209–44. See also Edwards' "Types of the Messiah," in *Works*, ed. Williams and Parsons, vol. 9, 401 f.

12 Edwards, *Images*, p. 44 (#8).

13 Ibid., p. 101 (#142).

14 Ibid., p. 96 (#124).

15 Ibid., p. 46 (#16).

16 Ibid., p. 79 (#79).

17 Jonathan Edwards, "The Nature of True Virtue," in *Works* ed. Williams and Parsons, p. 26.

18 Jonathan Edwards, "Miscellanies," #1296, quoted by Miller in his introduction to *Images* (p. 35) and mistakenly numbered 296.

19 Jonathan Edwards, "The Mind," in *The Philosophy of Jonathan Edwards from His Private Notebooks*, ed. Harvey G. Townsend (Eugene, 1955), p. 65 (#63).

20 Jonathan Edwards, "Covenant of Redemption: 'Excellency of Christ,' " in *Jonathan Edwards: Representative Selections*, ed. Clarence H. Faust and Thomas H. Johnson, rev. ed. (New York, 1962), p. 373.

21 Edwards, "Covenant of Redemption," pp. 372–73.

22 Ibid., p. 373.

23 Edwards, *The Nature of True Virtue*, ed. William K. Frankena (Ann Arbor, 1960), p. 28.

24 Jonathan Edwards, "Personal Narrative," in *Jonathan Edwards: A Profile,* ed. David Levin (New York, 1969), p. 27. Levin reprints Samuel Hopkin's *Life and Character of the Late Reverend Mr. Jonathan Edwards* (Boston, 1765), which includes the best currently available text of the "Personal Narrative."

25 Edwards, *Religious Affections,* p. 288.

26 *The Rambler* 4, no. 125 (London, 1752), p. 221. In context Johnson expounds upon the difficulty of defining literary genres, his point being that the imagination often frustrates analytical attempts at classification and definition, yet it produces works of art. His tone towards the subject appears to be ambivalent. The standard historical treatment of the imagination is Murray Wright Bundy's *The Theory of Imagination in Classical and Mediaeval Thought* (Urbana, 1928). A. S. P. Woodhouse has written an excellent brief survey of theories on the imagination, in *The Princeton Encyclopedia of Poetry and Poetics,* rev. ed. (Princeton, 1974), pp. 370–78, which includes a valuable bibliography. Ruth Leila Anderson in her *Elizabethan Psychology and Shakespeare's Plays* (New York, 1966) finds that "Elizabethan writers agree in describing this faculty [i.e., the imagination] as the general source of all our evils and disorderly passions . . . " (pp. 133–34). For discussion of the characteristic view of the English enlightenment, see Donald F. Bond, " 'Distrust' of Imagination in English Neo-Classicism," *Philological Quarterly* 14:54–69. Useful general discussions appear in R. L. Brett's *Fancy and Imagination* (London, 1969) and Wilma L. Kennedy's *The English Heritage of Coleridge of Bristol, 1798: The Basis in Eighteenth Century English Thought for His Distinction between Imagination and Fancy* (New York, 1969).

27 Thomas Hobbes, *The English Works of Thomas Hobbes of Malmesbury,* ed. Sir William Molesworth (London, 1839), vol. 3, p. 6.

28 Edwards, *Religious Affections,* pp. 285–86. See George Williamson, "The Restoration Revolt against Enthusiasm," *Studies in Philology* 30:571–603.

29 Edwards, *Religious Affections,* p. 286.

30 Quoted in ibid., p. 213; see also footnotes on pp. 213–17 and 289.

31 Ibid., pp. 290–91.

32 Ibid., p. 291.

33 Edwards, *The Great Awakening,* p. 236.

34 See Edwards, *Religious Affections,* p. 291.

35 Jonathan Edwards, "The Distinguishing Marks," in *The Great Awakening,* p. 237. Edwards made much the same point in "Some Thoughts Concerning the Revival" (p. 460 of the same volume):
Another thing that is often mixed with what is spiritual in the experiences of Christians are impressions on the imagination; whereby godly persons, together with a spiritual understanding of divine things and conviction of their reality and certainty, and a strong and deep sense of their excellency or great importance upon their hearts, have strongly impressed on their minds external ideas or images of things. A degree of imagination in such a case, as I have observed elsewhere, is unavoidable, and necessarily arises from human nature as constituted in the present state; and a degree of imagination is really useful, and often is of great benefit; but when it is in too great a degree it becomes an impure mixture that is prejudicial.

This mixture very often arises from the constitution of the body. It commonly greatly contributes to the other kind of mixture mentioned before, viz. of natural affections and passions; it helps to raise them to a great height.

36 Edwards, "A Faithful Narrative," p. 195.

37 Dwight, *The Life of President Edwards*, p. 178.

38 Edwards, "Personal Narrative," p. 27.

39 Edwards, "Covenant of Redemption," pp. 372–73.

40 John Locke, "A Letter Concerning Toleration," in *The Works of John Locke* (London, 1823), vol. 6, p. 6.

41 Hobbes, *English Works*, p. 17.

42 Dwight, *The Life of President Edwards*, pp. 703–04.

43 Edwards, "The Mind," p. 72.

44 Livingston Welch, *Imagination and Human Nature* (London, 1935), pp. 14f.

45 In "Jonathan Edwards on the Sense of the Heart," ed. Perry Miller, *Harvard Theological Review* 41:137.

46 Edwards, "Miscellanies," #238, in *The Philosophy of Jonathan Edwards from His Private Notebooks*, ed. Townsend, p. 248.

47 Dwight, *The Life of President Edwards*, p. 704.

48 Edwards, "A Faithful Narrative," p. 188.

49 "Sermon on 2 Cor. 13:5," quoted in Edwards, *Images*, pp. 31–32.

50 Edwards, *Works*, ed. Williams and Parsons, p. 211. Dwight, *The Life of President Edwards*, p. 601.

51 Dwight, *The Life of President Edwards*, p. 478, letter dated 28 Nov. 1751.

52 Edwards, "The Mind," p. 63 (#62).

53 See Edwards, "Miscellanies" #95, in Townsend, *The Philosophy of Jonathan Edwards*, p. 193; #153, #182, #188 in MS, Beinecke Rare Book and Manuscript Library, Yale University.

54 Edwards, *The Nature of True Virtue*, ed. Frankena, p. 28.

55 Edwards, *Religious Affections*, p. 114.

56 Ibid., p. 115.

57 The chapter to follow will touch upon the relation of Edwards' views on art to earlier Puritan aesthetics.

58 See Richard Crawford, "Watts for Singing: Metrical Poetry in American Sacred Tunebooks," *Early American Literature* 11:139–46.

59 Dwight, *The Life of President Edwards*, p. 177.

60 Ibid., p. 185.

61 See Thomas H. Johnson, "Jonathan Edwards' Background of Reading," *Publications of the Colonial Society of Massachusetts* 28:193–222; "Jonathan Edwards and the 'Young Folks' Bible,'" *New England Quarterly* 5:37–54. See also "Jonathan Edwards' 'Catalogue,'" ed. James S. Caskey (B.D. thesis, Chicago Theological Seminary, 1931).

62 Edwards, "Miscellanies," #251 in MS, Beinecke Rare Book and Manuscript Library, Yale University.

63 Ibid.

64 Edwards, "Covenant of Redemption," pp. 372–73.

65 Edwards, "Personal Narrative," pp. 26–28.
66 Ibid., p. 30. See "Miscellanies," #a in MS, Beinecke Rare Book and Manuscript Library, Yale University.
67 Perry Miller, *Jonathan Edwards* (New York, 1949), pp. 39, 201, 214.
68 See Wilson H. Kimnach, "Jonathan Edwards' Sermon Mill," *Early American Literature* 10:167–78.

Chapter 4

1 Jonathan Edwards, "A Faithful Narrative," in *The Great Awakening,* in The Works of Jonathan Edwards, Yale edition, vol. 4, ed. C. C. Goen (New Haven, 1957–), p. 188.
2 "Jonathan Edwards on the Sense of the Heart," ed. Perry Miller, *Harvard Theological Review* 41:139.
3 John Calvin, *Institutes of the Christian Religion,* ed. John T. McNeill (Philadelphia, 1960), vol. 1, pp. xi, 4.
4 John Cotton, *Some Treasures fetched out of Rubbish* (London, 1660), p. 23. Similar interdictions are to be found in William Ames, *The Marrow of Theology,* trans. and ed. John D. Eusden (Boston, 1968), p. 282; and in Samuel Willard, *A Compleat Body of Divinity* (1726; reprint, New York, 1969), p. 54.
5 See Allen I. Ludwig, *Graven Images: New England Stonecarving and Its Symbols, 1650–1815* (Middletown, Conn., 1966); Norman S. Grabo, "Puritan Devotion and American Literary History," in *Themes and Directions in American Literature: Essays in Honor of Leon Howard* (Lafayette, Indiana, 1969); John Phillips, *The Reformation of Images: Destruction of Art in England, 1535–1660* (Berkeley, 1974); Robert Daly, *God's Altar: The World and the Flesh in Puritan Poetry* (Berkeley, 1978); Lynn Haims, "The Face of God: Puritan Iconography in Early American Poetry, Sermons, and Tombstone Carving," *Early American Literature* 14:15–47.
6 Richard Baxter, *The Saints Everlasting Rest* (London, 1650), ch. xi, sec. 1, p. 756.
7 For discussion of Puritan attitudes towards meditation and their aesthetic import, see Kenneth Murdock, *Literature and Theology in Colonial New England* (Cambridge, 1949), p. 56; Lawrence A. Sasek, *The Literary Temper of the English Puritans* (Baton Rouge, 1961); Louis L. Martz, foreword to *The Poems of Edward Taylor,* ed. Donald E. Stanford (New Haven, 1960), and his *The Poetry of Meditation: A Study in English Religious Literature of the Seventeenth Century* (New Haven, 1954), especially chapter four, "Problems in Puritan Meditation: Richard Baxter"; Grabo, "Puritan Devotion and American Literary History"; and Daly, *God's Altar,* pp. 71–81.
8 Baxter, *The Saints Everlasting Rest,* pp. 756–60. Italics mine.
9 See Perry Miller, *The New England Mind: The Seventeenth Century* (Boston, 1961), pp. 300–62. Miller attributes the separation to the influence of Ramus. Daly, in *God's Altar,* challenges the assertion, arguing that Ramus' theories entailed no "theoretical compulsions" for poetry. "Had the Puritan poet considered his figures merely decorations, the products of his own mind and imagination, he

would have considered them and his poetry trivial," Daly claims, "but for the Puritan such figures and symbolic correspondences were not created by the rhetorician and therefore part of *elocutio*; they were created by God and found in the world by the poet" (pp. 54–55). In Daly's view the Puritans believed that a correspondence existed between spirit and nature, so that natural images served as divinely ordered types or symbols (Daly oddly equates the two) of spirit. Daly's case is weak. There is little evidence to support his objection to Miller. As we shall see in examining Baxter's comments and some other Puritan statements about images, the selection of figures would appear somewhat arbitrary, certainly not chosen as if fixed by divine contrivance.

10 Quoted in *The Puritans,* ed. Perry Miller and Thomas H. Johnson, rev. ed. (New York, 1963), vol. 2, p. 674.

11 *The Saints Dignitie and Dutie* (London, 1651), quoted in Babette May Levy's *Preaching in the First Half Century of New England History* (New York, 1945), p. 114. See Levy's informative discussion of Puritan use of similitudes, pp. 98–156; also, Phyllis Jones, "Biblical Rhetoric and the Pulpit Literature of Early New England," *Early American Literature* 11:245–58.

12 See Michael Wigglesworth's "A Short Discourse on Eternity," in *The Puritans,* ed. Miller and Johnson, vol. 2, pp. 606f.

13 Thomas Shepard, "The Sincere Convert," in *The Works of Thomas Shepard* (Boston, 1853; reprint, New York, 1967), vol. 1, p. 43.

14 Ibid., pp. 42–43.

15 Ibid., p. 35. Robert G. Collmer, "Two Antecedents for a Metaphor from Jonathan Edwards," *Notes and Queries* 201:396, finds two religious writers who previously employed the image of sinners hanging by a thread over the pit of hell: the fourteenth-century mystic Walter Hilton, in his *Scale of Perfection,* and the Counter-Reformer of the sixteenth century, Fray Luis de Granada in *Of Prayer and Meditation* (1554), translated into English from Spanish in 1582 by Richard Hopkins.

16 Willis J. Buckingham concludes in his "Stylistic Artistry in the Sermons of Jonathan Edwards," *Papers on Language and Literature* 6:150–51: "Unlike the typical Puritan divine. . . Edwards is not strikingly successful—in the great bulk of his sermons—in ornamenting his logic with arresting metaphors or homely examples. His strength lies in controlling the movement of language. It is in this sense that Edwards is indeed remarkable for naturalness; his style never seems artificial or merely pasted on. His rhetoric is always of the essence, not something separable and discrete. A mark of Edwards's achievement was the skill with which he successfully modified a mechanical, divisive Puritan aesthetic that tended to sever form from content."

17 Edwards, *The Great Awakening,* pp., 246–47. Italics mine.

18 Ibid., pp. 389–91.

19 Jonathan Edwards, in *Jonathan Edwards: Representative Selections,* ed. Clarence H. Faust and Thomas H. Johnson, rev. ed. (New York, 1962), p. 153.

20 Jonathan Edwards, "The Manner in Which the Salvation of the Soul Is To Be Sought," in *The Works of President Edwards,* ed. Edward Williams and Edward Parsons (London, 1817; reprint, New York, 1968), vol. 7, p. 378.

21 Edwards, *Representative Selections*, pp. 146–47.

22 Edwards, *Works,* ed. Williams and Parsons, vol. 7, p. 409.

23 Ibid., pp. 366–67.

24 Edwards, *Representative Selections, p.* 155.

25 Edwin H. Cady, "The Artistry of Jonathan Edwards," *New England Quarterly* 22:63. See also Buckingham, "Stylistic Artistry in the Sermons of Jonathan Edwards"; and Robert Lee Stuart, "Jonathan Edwards at Enfield: 'And Oh the Cheerfulness and Pleasantness . . . ,' " *American Literature* 48:46–59.

26 Edwards, *Representative Selections*, p. 156.

27 Benjamin Trumbull, *A Complete History of Connecticut, Civil and Ecclesiastical* (New Haven, 1818), vol. 2, p. 145.

28 Timothy Dwight, *Travels in New England and New York,* ed. B. M. Soloman (Cambridge, 1969), vol. 4, p. 230.

29 The fictional construct of the sermon, of course, turns upon more than imagery alone. There are other applications of the imagination, such as the fictitious report of the sinner in hell: "If we could speak with them [souls in hell], and inquire of them, one by one, whether they expected, when alive, and when they used to hear about hell, ever to be the subjects of that misery: we doubtless, should hear one and another reply, 'No, I never intended to come here: I had laid out matters otherwise in my mind: I thought I should contrive well for myself . . . ' " (p. 160). And there are conjectures, or imaginings, about, for instance, what the sinner will feel as he realizes that he must suffer for eternity (p. 169) and about the reactions of the congregation if some one of them were definitely known to be damned (p. 170).

30 Perry Miller, *Jonathan Edwards* (New York, 1949), p. 138.

31 John Griffith, "Jonathan Edwards as a Literary Artist," *Criticism, a Quarterly for Literature and the Arts* 15:160.

32 Thomas H. Johnson, "Jonathan Edwards and the 'Young Folks' Bible,' " *New England Quarterly* 5:39. Sasek, in *The Literary Temper of the English Puritans,* documents the traditional Puritan denunciation of romances (p. 59).

33 Sereno E. Dwight, *The Life of President Edwards,* vol. 1, The Works of President Edwards (New York, 1829), p. 601.

34 Generally the publication date is given as 1754, when all the books of the Richardson novel were in print. Johnson also accepts Dwight's anecdote without challenge in "Jonathan Edwards' Background of Reading," *Publications of the Colonial Society of Massachusetts* 28:216; and in his introduction to Edwards, *Representative Selections*, p. ciii; both in the main, of course, remain notable contributions to Edwards scholarship.

35 *The Scots Magazine* 11 (Nov. 1749), p. 538, reprinting the review from *Gentleman's Magazine,* claimed that *Clarissa* had "the first rank among romances." The manuscript of the "Catalogue" is in the Beinecke Rare Book and Manuscript Library, Yale University. I have used the transcription made by James Stillman Caskey, "Jonathan Edwards' 'Catalogue' " (B.D. thesis, Chicago Theological Seminary, 1931). Several of the entries on romances are also transcribed in Johnson's "Jonathan Edwards and the 'Young Folks' Bible' " and in his "Jonathan Edwards' Background of Reading," and in Franklin B. Dexter's "On the Manuscripts

of Jonathan Edwards," *Massachusetts Historical Society Proceedings*, 2nd. ser., 15:14–16, which contains extracts from the "Catalogue."

36 Johnson, "Jonathan Edwards' Background of Reading," pp. 203–06.

37 Ephraim Chambers, *Cyclopaedia: Or, an Universal Dictionary of Arts and Sciences* (London, 1738), vol. 2, s.v. "Romance."

38 Edwards, "A Faithful Narrative," p. 195.

39 The text of what is taken to be an apostrophe to Sarah Pierrepont is as follows:

> They say there is a young lady in [New Haven] who is beloved of that great Being who made and rules the world, and that there are certain seasons in which this great Being, in some way or other invisible, comes to her and fills her mind with exceeding sweet delight, and that she hardly cares for anything, except to meditate on him—that she expects after a while to be received up where he is, to be raised up out of the world and caught up into heaven; being assured that he loves her too well to let her remain at a distance from him always. There she is to dwell with him, and to be ravished with his love and delight forever.... She has a strange sweetness in her mind, and singular purity in her affections; is most just and conscientious in all her conduct; and you could not persuade her to do anything wrong or sinful, if you would give her all the world, lest she should offend this great Being. She is of a wonderful sweetness, calmness and universal benevolence of mind; especially after this great God has manifested himself to her mind.... She loves to be alone, walking in the fields and groves, and seems to have someone invisible always conversing with her.

From C. C. Goen's introduction to Edwards, *The Great Awakening*, p. 68.

40 Norman Grabo, "The Veiled Vision: The Role of Aesthetics in Early American Intellectual History," *William and Mary Quarterly* 19:508.

41 Miller, *Jonathan Edwards*, p. 202.

42 Ibid., p. 201.

Chapter 5

1 Alan Heimert, *Religion and the American Mind* (Cambridge, 1966), pp. 6, 52, 103.

2 Roland A. Delattre, "Beauty and Politics: A Problematic Legacy of Jonathan Edwards," in *American Philosophy from Edwards to Quine*, ed. Robert W. Shahan and Kenneth R. Merrill (Norman, Oklahoma, 1977), p. 23.

3 I hope at a later date to analyze in greater depth and with adequate documentation the topics broached here to suggest some of the implications of the present study. A comprehensive definition of the Puritan tradition in American literature is still lacking; the present chapter, it is hoped, will indicate some of its facets, especially those that Edwards may have contributed or reinforced.

4 Williston Walker, respected historian of religion in New England, claimed that "*The Nature of True Virtue*,—though incomplete, expresses in metaphysical form the feature of the teaching of Edwards that has probably most affected New Eng-

land thought." That feature, according to Walker, is that "virtue is benevolence, or love to intelligent being in proportion to the amount of being which each personality possesses." In *Ten New England Leaders* (1901; reprint, New York, 1969), p. 255. The student of literature should remember that *True Virtue* presents Edwards' conception of secondary beauty, according to which natural beauty, typologically, parallels spiritual beauty, functioning as a vehicle to serve comprehension.

5 Sidney Earl Mead, *Nathaniel William Taylor, 1786–1858: A Connecticut Liberal* (1942; reprint, n.p., 1967), p. 16.

6 Robert L. Ferm, *A Colonial Pastor, Jonathan Edwards the Younger: 1745–1801* (Grand Rapids, 1976), pp. 62–63. See also Joseph Haroutunian, *Piety versus Moralism: The Passing of the New England Theology* (New York, 1932); George N. Boardman, *A History of the New England Theology* (New York, 1899); and Sydney E. Ahlstrom, *A Religious History of the American People* (Garden City, New York, 1975), vol. 1, pp. 489–503.

7 Calvin Ellis Stowe, letter to George Eliot, 1870, quoted in Charles Edward Stowe, *Life of Harriet Beecher Stowe* (Boston, 1890), pp. 574–75; "Sketches and Recollections of Dr. Lyman Beecher," in *The Congregational Quarterly* 6:224.

8 Harriet Beecher Stowe, *The Minister's Wooing* (New York, 1959), p. 88. Henry F. May contributes an insightful and well-documented view of Stowe's attitude towards and depiction of, her inherited Calvinist tradition in his introduction to her *Oldtown Folks* (Cambridge, 1966). See also Charles H. Foster's *The Rungless Ladder: Harriet Beecher Stowe and New England Puritanism* (Durham, 1954).

9 William Ellery Channing, "Christian Worship: Discourse at the Dedication of the Unitarian Church, Newport, Rhode Island, July 27, 1836," in *The Works of William E. Channing, D.D.* (Boston, 1882), pp. 423, 425.

10 Oliver Wendell Elsbree, "Samuel Hopkins and His Doctrine of Benevolence," *New England Quarterly* 8:540, remarks that by teaching that holiness is the essence of God and that it consists of benevolence, Hopkins modified significantly the Edwardsian principle of true virtue. Edwards had said that benevolence is the sum total of the attributes of God, while Hopkins, claims Elsbree, taught that benevolence *is* God; the distinction, he says, may have an as yet uncalculated import in the development of Transcendentalism. Unfortunately to pursue Elsbree's suggestion would require an exploration of the meaning of the *ideal* in nineteenth-century New England thought, a complex undertaking, which intellectual historians peculiarly seem to have avoided, though reference to *ideals* abound (the notion of idealism from a philosophic, epistemological perspective has frequently been analyzed in commentaries on the history of American philosophy—another subject altogether, or nearly so).

11 Kenneth B. Murdock, "The Puritan Tradition in American Literature," in *The Reinterpretation of American Literature: Some Contributions toward the Understanding of Its Historical Development*, ed. Norman Foerster (New York, 1959), p. 101.

12 Perry Miller, "From Edwards to Emerson," in *Errand into the Wilderness* (Cambridge, 1956), p. 192. The essay originally appeared in *New England Quarterly* 13:589–617. Subsequently Rene Wellek argued that the origins of American

Transcendentalism were not to be found in nineteenth-century German idealism: "The Transcendentalists were merely looking for corroboration of their faith. They found it in Germany, but ultimately they did not need this confirmation. Their faith was deeply rooted in their minds and their own spiritual ancestry." From "Emerson and Germany Philosophy," *New England Quarterly* 16:62.

13 Ursula Brumm, *American Thought and Religious Typology* (New Brunswick, N.J., 1970), p. 102. See chapter six, "Jonathan Edwards and Ralph Waldo Emerson," pp. 86–238.

14 William A. Clebsch, *American Religious Thought, A History* (Chicago, 1973), p. xvi.

15 Ibid., p. 55. Another commentary that should be noted is William L. Hedges' thoughtful "From Franklin to Emerson," in *The Oldest Revolutionary, Essays on Benjamin Franklin*, ed. J. A. Leo Lemay (Philadelphia, 1976), pp. 139–56. Hedges observes that the formulation of the Puritan tradition that pits the practicality of Benjamin Franklin, as a foil, against the piety of Edwards and Emerson ignores the point at which "piety and practicality merge" (p. 144).

16 Ralph Waldo Emerson, "Humanity of Science," in *The Early Lectures of Ralph Waldo Emerson*, ed. Stephen E. Whicher and Robert E. Spiller (Cambridge, 1959), vol. 2, p. 22. The lecture was delivered on Dec. 22, 1836.

17 In Merton M. Sealts, Jr., and Alfred R. Ferguson, eds., *Emerson's Nature—Origin, Growth, Meaning* (New York, 1969), p. 18.

18 Ralph Waldo Emerson, "Natural History of Intellect," in *Works* (Boston, 1904), vol. 12, p. 37.

19 Emerson, *Early Lectures*, vol. 2, pp. 99–100.

20 "The Over-Soul," in *The American Tradition in Literature*, 3rd ed., ed. Sculley Bradley, et al. (New York, 1967), vol. 1, pp. 1162–63.

21 Ralph Waldo Emerson, "The Heart," in *Early Lectures*, vol. 2, pp. 293–94.

22 Ibid., p. 282.

23 Ralph Waldo Emerson, "Ethics," in *Early Lectures*, vol. 2, p. 154.

24 Sealts and Ferguson, *Emerson's Nature*, p. 14.

25 Ralph Waldo Emerson, "The Relation of Man to the Globe," in *Early Lectures*, vol. 1, pp. 48–49.

26 Ralph Waldo Emerson, "The Miracle of Our Being," in *Young Emerson Speaks: Unpublished Discourses on Many Subjects*, ed. Arthur Cushman McGiffert, Jr. (Boston, 1938), p. 211.

27 Ralph Waldo Emerson, "Art," in *Early Lectures*, vol, 2, pp. 44–45.

28 Emerson, "The Miracle of Our Being," p. 210.

29 See John Calvin's *Institutes of the Christian Religion*, ed. John T. McNeill, trans. Ford Lewis Battles (Philadelphia, 1960), vol. 1, chap. iii, sec. vii ("The Sum of the Christian Life: The Denial of Ourselves").

30 Stowe, *The Minister's Wooing*, pp. 24–25.

31 Stowe, *The Minister's Wooing*, pp. 121–22. Stowe quotes (p. 315) Edwards' remarks in *The Religious Affections* on the *earnest*.

32 Emerson, "Art," p. 50.

Selective Bibliography

I. Primary Sources of Jonathan Edwards

The Works of Jonathan Edwards. General editor, John E. Smith. New Haven, 1957–.
   Vol. 1, *The Freedom of the Will*, edited by Paul Ramsey. Vol. 2, *Religious Affec-*
   tions, edited by John E. Smith. Vol. 3, *Original Sin*, edited by Clyde Holbrook.
   Vol. 4, *The Great Awakening*, edited by C. C. Goen.
The Works of President Edwards. Edited by Edward Williams and Edward Parsons.
   10 vols. London, 1817; reprint, New York, 1968.
The Works of President Edwards. Edited by Sereno E. Dwight. 10 vols. New York,
   1829–30.
The Works of President Edwards. 4 vols. New York, 1849.

Images or Shadows of Divine Things. Edited by Perry Miller. New Haven, 1948.
"Jonathan Edwards' 'Catalogue.' " Edited by James S. Caskey. B.D. thesis, Chicago
   Theological Seminary, 1931.
"Jonathan Edwards on the Sense of the Heart." Edited by Perry Miller. *Harvard The-*
   ological Review, 41(1948):123–45.
Jonathan Edwards: A Profile. Edited by David Levin. New York, 1969.
Jonathan Edwards: Representative Selections. Rev. ed. Edited by Clarence H. Faust
   and Thomas H. Johnson. New York, 1962.
"The Mind" of Jonathan Edwards: A Reconstructed Text. Edited by Leon Howard.
   Berkeley, 1963.
"Miscellanies." Transcribed by Thomas A. Schafer. Beinecke Rare Book and Manu-
   script Library, Yale University.
The Nature of True Virtue. Edited by William K. Frankena. Ann Arbor, 1960.
The Philosophy of Jonathan Edwards from His Private Notebooks. Edited by Harvey
   G. Townsend. Eugene, 1955.
Treatise on Grace and Other Posthumously Published Writings. Edited by Paul
   Helm. London, 1971.

II. Bibliographies

Burggraaff, Winfield J. "Jonathan Edwards: A Bibliographical Essay." *Reformed Review* 18(1965):19–33.

"Checklist of Doctoral Dissertations on American Presbyterian and Reformed Subjects, 1912–1965, A." *Journal of Presbyterian History* 45(1967):203–21.

Emerson, Everett H. "Jonathan Edwards." In *Fifteen American Authors Before 1900: Bibliographic Essays on Research and Criticism*, pp. 169–84. Edited by R. A. Rees and E. N. Harbert. Madison, 1971.

Faust, Clarence H., and Johnson, Thomas H. "Introduction." *Jonathan Edwards: Representative Selections*. Rev. ed. New York, 1962.

Johnson, Thomas. *The Printed Writings of Jonathan Edwards, 1703–1758: A Bibliography*. Princeton, 1940.

McGiffert, Michael. "American Puritan Studies in the 1960s." *William and Mary Quarterly*, 3rd ser., 27(1970):36–67.

Sliwoski, Richard S. "Doctoral Dissertations on Jonathan Edwards." *Early American Literature* 14:3 (Winter 1979–80): 318–27.

U. S. Library of Congress. "A List of Printed Materials [on] Jonathan Edwards, 1703–1758, to be Found in the U. S. Library of Congress Reading Room, including Biographies, Appreciations, Criticisms, and Fugitive References." Washington, D.C., 1934.

Werge, Thomas. "Jonathan Edwards and the Puritan Mind in America: Directions in Textual and Interpretive Criticism." *Reformed Review* 28(1970):153–65, 173–83.

III. Miscellaneous

Aldridge, A. Owen. "Edwards and Hutcheson." *Harvard Theological Review* 44(1951):35–53.

Alexander, Archibald. *Theories of the Will in the History of Philosophy*. New York, 1898.

Allen, Alexander V. G. *Jonathan Edwards*. Boston, 1889.

Ames, William. *The Marrow of Theology*. Translated by John D. Eusden. Boston, 1968.

Anderson, Ruth Leila. *Elizabethan Psychology and Shakespeare's Plays*. New York, 1966.

Angoff, Charles, ed. *Jonathan Edwards: His Life and Influence, Papers and Discussions by Conrad Cherry, Wilson H. Kimnach, Charles Wetzel, Donald Jones, Edward Cook*. Rutherford, New Jersey, 1975.

Augustine. *Concerning the City of God against the Pagans*. Translated by Henry Bettenson. London, 1972.

———. *Confessions*. Translated by William Watts. London, 1968.

Baumgartner, Paul R. "Jonathan Edwards: The Theory Behind His Use of Figurative Language." *Publications of the Modern Language Association of America* 78(1963):321–25.

Baxter, Richard. *The Saints Everlasting Rest.* London, 1650.

Becker, William Hartshorne. "The Distinguishing Marks of the Christian Man in the Thought of Jonathan Edwards." Ph.D. dissertation, Harvard University, 1964.

Berner, Robert L. "Grace and Works in America: The Role of Jonathan Edwards." *The Southern Quarterly* 15(1977):125–34.

Bond, Donald F. " 'Distrust' of Imagination in English Neo-Classicism." *Philological Quarterly* 14(1935):54–69.

Bourke, Vernon J. *Will in Western Thought: An Historico-Critical Survey.* New York, 1964.

Bradley, Sculley, et al., eds. *The American Tradition in Literature.* 3rd ed. New York, 1967.

Brett, R. L. *Fancy and Imagination.* London, 1969.

Brumm, Ursula. "Jonathan Edwards and Ralph Waldo Emerson." In *American Thought and Religious Typology.* New Brunswick, N.J., 1970.

Buckingham, Willis J. "Stylistic Artistry in the Sermons of Jonathan Edwards." *Papers on Language and Literature* 6(1970): 136–51.

Bundy, Murray Wright. *The Theory of Imagination in Classical and Mediaeval Thought.* Urbana, 1928.

Bushman, Richard L. *From Puritan to Yankee: Character and the Social Order in Connecticut, 1690–1765.* Cambridge, 1967.

Cady, Edwin H. "The Artistry of Jonathan Edwards." *New England Quarterly* 22(1949):61–72.

Calvin, John. *Corpus Reformatorum: Ioannis Calvini, Opera Quae Supersunt Omnia.* Edited by G. Baum, E. Cunitz, and E. Reuss. Brunswick, Germany, 1863. Vols. 2, 3, and 4.

———. *The Institutes of the Christian Religion.* Translated by Thomas Norton. London, 1561.

———. *Institutes of the Christian Religion.* Translated by John Allen. London, 1813.

———. *The Institutes of the Christian Religion.* Translated by Henry Beveridge. Edinburgh, 1845.

———. *Institutes of the Christian Religion.* Edited by John T. McNeill. Translated by Ford Lewis Battles. Philadelphia, 1960.

Carpenter, Frederick Ives. "The Radicalism of Jonathan Edwards." *New England Quarterly* 4(1931):629–44.

Carse, James. *Jonathan Edwards and the Visibility of God.* New York, 1967.

Chambers, Ephraim. *Cyclopaedia: Or, an Universal Dictionary of Arts and Sciences.* 2 vols. London, 1738.

"Character of *Clarissa*, A." *The Scots Magazine* 11 (Nov.1749):538–44.

Cherry, Conrad. *The Theology of Jonathan Edwards: A Reappraisal.* Garden City, New York, 1966.

Colacurcio, Michael J. "The Example of Edwards: Idealist Imagination and the Metaphysics of Sovereignty." In *Puritan Influences in American Literature.* Edited by Emory Elliott. Urbana, 1979.

Collmer, Robert G. "Two Antecedents for a Metaphor from Jonathan Edwards." *Notes and Queries* 201(Sept. 1956):396.

Confession of Faith, The. Inverness, Scotland, 1970.

Cotton, John. *Some Treasures fetched out of Rubbish.* London, 1660.

Crabtree, Arthur B. *Jonathan Edwards' View of Man: A Study in Eighteenth Century Calvinism.* Wallington, England, 1948.

Craig, Samuel G., ed. *Calvin and Augustine.* Philadelphia, 1956.

Crawford, Richard. "Watts for Singing: Metrical Poetry in American Sacred Tunebooks." *Early American Literature* 11(Fall 1976):139–46.

Daly, Robert. *God's Altar: The World and the Flesh in Puritan Poetry.* Berkeley, 1978.

Davidson, Edward H. "From Locke to Edwards." *Journal of the History of Ideas* 24(1963):355–72.

Delattre, Roland A. "Beauty and Politics: A Problematic Legacy of Jonathan Edwards." In Robert Shahan and Kenneth Merrill, eds. *American Philosophy from Edwards to Quine.* Norman, Okla., 1977.

———. *Beauty and Sensibility in the Thought of Jonathan Edwards: An Essay in Aesthetics and Theological Ethics.* New Haven, 1968.

Dexter, Franklin B. "On the Manuscripts of Jonathan Edwards." *Massachusetts Historical Society Proceedings,* 2nd ser., 15(1902):2–16.

Dexter, Henry M. *The Congregationalism of the Last Three Hundred Years as Seen in Its Literature.* New York, 1880.

Dingley, Robert. *The Spiritual Taste Described and a Glimpse of Christ Discovered.* London, 1649.

Dodds, Elisabeth D. *Marriage to a Difficult Man: The "Uncommon Union" of Jonathan and Sarah Edwards.* Philadelphia, 1971.

Dowey, E. A., Jr. *The Knowledge of God in Calvin's Theology.* New York, 1952.

Dwight, Sereno E. *The Life of President Edwards.* Vol. 1 of The Works of President Edwards. New York, 1829

Dwight, Timothy. *Travels in New England and New York.* Edited by B. M. Soloman. 4 vols. Cambridge, 1969.

Elliott, Emory. *Power and the Pulpit in Puritan New England.* Princeton, 1975.

Elwood, Douglas J. *The Philosophical Theology of Jonathan Edwards.* New York, 1960.

Emerson, Everett. *English Puritanism from John Hooper to John Milton.* Durham, 1968.

Emerson, Ralph Waldo. *The Early Lectures of Ralph Waldo Emerson.* Edited by Stephen E. Whicher and Robert E. Spiller. Cambridge, 1959.

———. *Works.* Boston, 1904.

———. *Young Emerson Speaks: Unpublished Discourses on Many Subjects.* Edited by Arthur Cushman McGiffert, Jr. Boston, 1938.

Fenner, William. *Works.* London, 1657.

Fiering, Norman S. "Will and Intellect in the New England Mind." *William and Mary Quarterly,* 3rd. ser., 29(1972):515–58.

Fisher, George Park. *History of Christian Doctrine.* New York, 1896.

———. "The Philosophy of Jonathan Edwards." *North American Review* 128 (1879):284–303.

Fulcher, J. Rodney. "Puritans and the Passions: The Faculty Psychology in American Puritanism." *Journal of the History of the Behavioral Sciences* 9(1973): 123–39.

Gohdes, Clarence. "Aspects of Idealism in Early New England." *Philosophical Review* 39(1930):537–55.

Goodwin, Gerald J. "The Myth of 'Arminian-Calvinism' in Eighteenth Century New England." *New England Quarterly* 41(1968):213–37.

Grabo, Norman. "Puritan Devotion and American Literary History." In *Themes and Directions in American Literature, Essays in Honor of Leon Howard*. Edited by Ray B. Browne and Donald Pizer. Lafayette, 1969.

———. "The Veiled Vision: The Role of Aesthetics in Early American Intellectual History." *William and Mary Quarterly* 19(1962):493–510.

Griffin, Edward M. *Jonathan Edwards*. Minneapolis, 1971.

Griffith, John. "Jonathan Edwards as a Literary Artist." *Criticism, a Quarterly for Literature and the Arts* 15(1973):156–73.

Haims, Lynn. "The Face of God: Puritan Iconography in Early American Poetry, Sermons, and Tombstone Carving." *Early American Literature* 14(Spring 1979): 15–47.

Hall, Basil. "Puritanism: The Problem of Definition." In *Studies in Church History, II*, pp. 283–96. Edited by G. J. Cuming. London, 1965.

Hall, David. D. *The Faithful Shepherd: A History of the New England Ministry in the Seventeenth Century*. Chapel Hill, 1972.

———. "Understanding the Puritans." In *The State of American History*, pp. 330–49. Edited by Herbert J. Bass. Chicago, 1970.

Haroutunian, Joseph. *Piety Versus Moralism: The Passing of the New England Theology*. New York, 1932.

Hedges, William L. "From Franklin to Emerson." In *The Oldest Revolutionary, Essays on Benjamin Franklin*. Edited by J. A. Leo Lemay. N. p., 1976.

Heimert, Alan. *Religion and the American Mind*. Cambridge, 1966.

Helm, Paul. "John Locke and Jonathan Edwards: A Reconsideration." *Journal of the History of Philosophy* 7(1969):51–61.

Heppe, Heinrich. *Reformed Dogmatics*. London, 1950.

Hitchcock, Orville A. "A Critical Study of the Oratorical Technique of Jonathan Edwards." Ph.D. dissertation, University of Iowa, 1936.

———. "Jonathan Edwards." In *A History and Criticism of American Public Address*, vol. 1, pp. 213–37. Edited by William Norwood Brigance. 3 vols. New York, 1943.

Hobbes, Thomas. *Leviathan*. Vol. 1: *The English Works of Thomas Hobbes of Malmesbury*. Edited by Sir William Molesworth. London, 1839.

Holbrook, Clyde A. *The Ethics of Jonathan Edwards: Morality and Aesthetics*. Ann Arbor, 1973.

———. "Jonathan Edwards and His Detractors." *Theology Today* 10(1953): 384–96.

Hooker, Thomas. *The Application of Redemption*. London, 1656.

———. *The Soules Implantation*. London, 1637.

Horton, Douglas, ed. and trans. *William Ames by Matthew Nethenus, Hugo Visscher, and Karl Reuter.* Cambridge, 1965.

Howell, Wilbur Samuel. *Logic and Rhetoric in England, 1500–1700.* Princeton, 1956.

Hubbell, Jay B. *Who Are the Major American Writers? A Study of the Changing Literary Canon.* Durham, 1972.

Hudson, Winthrop S. "The Morison Myth Concerning the Founding of Harvard College." *Church History* 8(1939):148–59.

Johnson, Thomas H. "Jonathan Edwards." In *Literary History of the United States,* pp. 71–81. Edited by Robert E. Spiller, et al. 3rd ed. London, 1963.

———. "Jonathan Edwards and the 'Young Folks' Bible.'" *New England Quarterly* 5(1932):37–54.

———. "Jonathan Edwards' Background of Reading." *Publications of the Colonial Society of Massachusetts* 28(1931):193–222.

Jones, Phyllis. "Biblical Rhetoric and the Pulpit Literature of Early New England." *Early American Literature* 11(Winter 1976):245–58.

Kennedy, Wilma L. *The English Heritage of Coleridge of Bristol, 1798: The Basis in Eighteenth Century English Thought for His Distinction between Imagination and Fancy.* New York, 1969.

Kimnach, Wilson H. "Jonathan Edwards' Sermon Mill." *Early American Literature* 10(Fall 1975):167–78.

———. "The Literary Techniques of Jonathan Edwards." Ph.D. dissertation, University of Pennsylvania, 1971.

Knappen, M. M. *Tudor Puritanism: A Chapter in the History of Idealism.* Chicago, 1939.

———. *Two Elizabethan Puritan Diaries.* Chicago, 1933.

Kolodny, Annette. "Imagery in the Sermons of Jonathan Edwards." *Early American Literature* 7(Fall 1972):172–82.

Lee, Marc Frank. "A Literary Approach to Selected Writings of Jonathan Edwards." Ph.D. dissertation, University of Wisconsin/Milwaukee, 1973.

Lee, Sang Hyun. "Jonathan Edwards' Theory of the Imagination." *Michigan Academic* 5(1972):233–41.

———. "Mental Activity and the Perception of Beauty in Jonathan Edwards." *Harvard Theological Review* 69(1976):369–96.

Levy, Babette May. *Preaching in the First Half Century of New England History.* New York, 1945.

Lewis, R. W. B. "The Drama of Jonathan Edwards." Review of *Jonathan Edwards* by Perry Miller. *The Hudson Review* 3(1950):135–40.

Locke, John. *An Essay Concerning Human Understanding.* Edited by Alexander Campbell Fraser. 2 vols. New York, 1959.

———. *The Works of John Locke.* 10 vols. London, 1823.

Lowance, Mason I., Jr. "'Images or Shadows of Divine Things' in the Thought of Jonathan Edwards." In *Typology and Early American Literature,* pp. 209–44. Edited by Sacvan Bercovitch. Amherst, 1972.

Lucas, Paul R. *Valley of Discord: Church and Society along the Connecticut River, 1636–1725.* Hanover, New Hampshire, 1976.

Ludwig, Allan I. *Graven Images: New England Stonecarving and Its Symbols, 1650–1815.* Middletown, Conn., 1966.

Lyttle, David. "Jonathan Edwards on Personal Identity." *Early American Literature* 7(Fall 1972):163–71.

———. "The Sixth Sense of Jonathan Edwards." *Church Quarterly Review* 167 (1966):50–59.

McGiffert, Michael, ed. *Puritanism and the American Experience.* Reading, Massachusetts, 1969.

McNeill, John T. *The History and Character of Calvinism.* New York, 1954.

Martin, Howard H. "Ramus, Ames, Perkins and Colonial Rhetoric." *Western Speech* 23(1959):74–82.

Martz, Louis L. Foreword to *The Poems of Edward Taylor.* Edited by Donald E. Stanford. New Haven, 1960.

———. *The Poetry of Meditation: A Study in English Religious Literature of the Seventeenth Century.* New Haven, 1954.

Middlekauff, Robert. "Piety and Intellect in Puritanism." *William and Mary Quarterly,* 3rd ser., 22(1965):457–70.

Miller, Perry. "Benjamin Franklin, Jonathan Edwards." In *Major Writers of America,* pp. 83–94. Edited by Newton Arvin, et al. New York, 1962.

———. *Jonathan Edwards.* New York, 1949.

———. *The New England Mind: The Seventeenth Century.* Boston, 1961.

———. "The Rhetoric of Sensation." In *Errand into the Wilderness,* pp. 167–83. Cambridge, 1964.

Miller, Perry and Johnson, Thomas H., eds. *The Puritans.* Rev. ed. New York, 1963.

Morgan, Edmund S. *The Puritan Dilemma: The Story of John Winthrop.* Boston, 1958.

———. *Visible Saints: The History of a Puritan Idea.* New York, 1963.

Murdock, Kenneth B. *Literature and Theology in Colonial New England.* Cambridge, 1949.

———. "The Puritan Tradition in American Literature." In *The Reinterpretation of American Literature: Some Contributions toward the Understanding of Its Historical Development,* pp. 83–113. Edited by Norman Foerster and Robert P. Falk. New York, 1959.

New, John F. H. *Anglican and Puritan: The Basis of Their Opposition, 1558–1640.* Stanford, 1964.

Newlin, Claude M. *Philosophy and Religion in Colonial America.* New York, 1962.

Newton, Sir Isaac. *The Mathematical Principles of Natural Philosophy.* Translated by Andrew Motte. 2 vols. London, 1968.

———. *Opticks, or A Treatise of the Reflections, Refractions, Inflections and Colours of Light.* New York, 1952.

Nuttall, Geoffrey. *The Holy Spirit in Puritan Faith and Experience.* Oxford, 1947.

Oviatt, Edwin. *The Beginnings of Yale (1701–1726).* New Haven, 1916.

Perkins, William. *William Perkins, 1558–1602, English Puritanist.* Edited by Thomas F. Merrill. The Hague, The Netherlands, 1966.

"Perry Miller and the American Mind, a Memorial Issue." *Harvard Review* 2(1964).

Pettit, Norman. *The Heart Prepared: Grace and Conversion in Puritan Spiritual Life.* New Haven, 1966.

Powell, Vavasor. *Spirituall Experiences of Sundry Beleevers.* London, 1652.

Preston, John. *The New Covenant.* 9th ed., rev. London, 1639.

Rogers, Jack Bartlett. *Scripture in the Westminster Confession: A Problem of Historical Interpretation for American Presbyterianism.* Grand Rapids, 1967.

Sasek, Lawrence A. *The Literary Temper of the English Puritans.* Baton Rouge, 1961.

Schafer, Thomas. "The Concept of Being in the Thought of Jonathan Edwards." Ph.D. dissertation, Duke University, 1951.

———. "Jonathan Edwards and Justification by Faith." *Church History* 20(1951): 55–67.

———. "Jonathan Edwards' Conception of the Church." *Church History* 24(1955): 51–66.

———. "Manuscript Problems in the Yale Edition of Jonathan Edwards." *Early American Literature* 3(Winter 1968–69):159–71.

Schieck, William J. *The Will and the Word: The Poetry of Edward Taylor.* Athens, Georgia, 1974.

———.*The Writings of Jonathan Edwards: Theme, Motif, and Style.* College Station, Texas, 1975.

Schlaeger, Margaret. "Jonathan Edwards's Theory of Perception." Ph.D. dissertation, University of Illinois, 1964.

Schneider, Herbert W. *A History of American Philosophy.* New York, 1946.

Sealts, Merton M., Jr., and Ferguson, Alfred R., eds. *Emerson's Nature—Origin, Growth, Meaning.* New York, 1969.

Shea, Daniel B. "The Art and Instruction of Jonathan Edwards' *Personal Narrative.*" *American Literature* 37(March 1965):17–32.

———. *Spiritual Autobiography in Early America.* Princeton, 1968.

Shepard, Thomas. *God's Plot: The Paradoxes of Puritan Piety, Being the Autobiography and Journal of Thomas Shepard.* Edited by Michael McGiffert. Amherst, 1972.

———. *The Works of Thomas Shepard.* 3 vols. Boston, 1853; reprint, New York, 1967.

Sibbes, Richard. *The Complete Works.* Edited by Alexander Grosart. Edinburgh, 1862.

Simonson, Harold. *Jonathan Edwards: Theologian of the Heart.* Grand Rapids, 1974.

———, ed. *Selected Writings of Jonathan Edwards.* New York, 1970.

Smith, Claude A. "Jonathan Edwards and 'the Way of Ideas.' " *Harvard Theological Review* 59(1966):153–73.

Smith, John. *Select Discourses.* Edited by Henry Griffin Williams. Cambridge, England, 1859.

Smith, John E. Editor's introduction to *Religious Affections,* by Jonathan Edwards. New Haven, 1959.

Stein, Stephen J. "Jonathan Edwards and the Rainbow: Biblical Exegesis and Poetic

Imagination." *New England Quarterly* 47(Sept. 1974):440–56.

Stoddard, Solomon. *Safety of Appearing*. Boston, 1729.

Stoughton, John A. *Windsor Farmes: A Glimpse of an Old Parish*. Hartford, 1883.

Stuart, Robert Lee. "Jonathan Edwards at Enfield: 'And Oh the Cheerfulness and Pleasantness. . . .' " *American Literature* 48(March 1976):46–59.

Tomas, Vincent. "The Modernity of Jonathan Edwards." *New England Quarterly* 25(1952):60–84.

Townsend, Harvey Gates. "The Will and the Understanding in the Philosophy of Jonathan Edwards." *Church History* 16(1947):210–20.

Trinterud, Leonard J. *The Forming of an American Tradition: A Re-Examination of Colonial Presbyterianism*. Philadelphia, 1949.

Trumbull, Benjamin. *History of Connecticut*. 2 vols. New Haven, 1818.

van Beek, M. *An Enquiry into Puritan Vocabulary*. Groningen, The Netherlands, 1969.

van Mastricht, Peter. *A Treatise on Regeneration, Extracted from His System of Divinity Called Theologia-Practica; And Faithfully Translated into English; with an Appendix, Containing Extracts from Many Celebrated Divines of the Reformed Church, upon the Same Subject*. New Haven, [1770].

von Rohr, John. "Covenant and Assurance in Early English Puritanism." *Church History* 34(June 1965):195–203.

Warfield, B. B. "Edwards and the New England Theology." In *Encyclopaedia of Religion and Ethics*, vol. 5, pp. 221–27. Edited by James Hastings. New York, 1928.

Watkins, Owen C. *The Puritan Experience: Studies in Spiritual Autobiography*. New York, 1972.

Watts, Emily S. "Jonathan Edwards and the Cambridge Platonists." Ph.D. dissertation, University of Illinois, 1963.

———. "The Neoplatonic Basis of Jonathan Edwards' 'True Virtue.' " *Early American Literature* 10(Fall 1975):179–89.

Welch, Livingston. *Imagination and Human Nature*. London, 1935.

Wencelius, L. *L'Esthetique de Calvin*. Paris, 1937.

White, Morton. *Science and Sentiment in America: Philosophical Thought from Jonathan Edwards to John Dewey*. New York, 1972.

Whittemore, Robert C. "Jonathan Edwards and the Theology of the Sixth Way." *Church History* 35(March 1966):60–65.

Williamson, George. "The Restoration Revolt against Enthusiasm." *Studies in Philology* 30(1933):571–603.

Winslow, Ola Elizabeth. *Jonathan Edwards, 1703–1758: A Biography*. New York, 1940.

Wise, Gene. "Implicit Irony in Recent American Historiography: Perry Miller's New England." *Journal of the History of Ideas* 29(1968):579–600.

Wollebius, John. *The Abridgement of Christian Divinity*. Translated by Alexander Ross. London, 1656.

Woodhouse, A. S. P. "Imagination." In *The Princeton Encyclopedia of Poetry and Poetics*. Rev. ed. Princeton, 1974.

Wright, Conrad. *The Beginnings of Unitarianism in America*. Boston, 1955.

Yates, Frances A. *The Art of Memory*. Chicago, 1966.

Index

Library of Congress Cataloging in Publication Data
Erdt, Terrence, 1942–
Jonathan Edwards, art and the sense of the heart.
Bibliography: p.
Includes index.
1. Edwards, Jonathan, 1703–1758—Aesthetics.
2. Aesthetics. I. Title.
B874.A4E72   111'.85   80–5380
ISBN 0–87023–304–1